Love, Beauty
& the Divine Feminine

AWAKENING
to
APHRODITE'S
LIGHT

Love, Beauty
& the Divine Feminine

AWAKENING
to
APHRODITE'S
LIGHT

Geraldine S. Brooks

WONDERWELL

Published by Wonderwell Press
Austin, Texas
www.gbgpress.com

Distributed by River Grove Books

Design and composition by Greenleaf Book Group and Mimi Bark
Cover design by Greenleaf Book Group and Mimi Bark
Cover images used under license from ©Shutterstock.com/sumon sharif

Publisher's Cataloging-in-Publication data is available.

Print ISBN: 978-1-963827-14-9

eBook ISBN: 978-1-963827-15-6

First Edition

In loving memory of my mother

AGNES

&

For my beautiful goddaughter

ANGELICA

Contents

Acknowledgments   ix

Introduction: Meeting the Goddess of Love and Beauty   1

1: Awakening to Aphrodite in Our Wounded World   11

2: Who Is Aphrodite?   25

3: She Is the Golden One / She Is the Dark One   53

4: Aphrodite's Transformative Powers   69

5: Eros, Sex, and Desire   79

6: Let's Talk About Beauty   101

7: Beauty's Opposition   121

8: Love, Beauty, and the Senses   141

9: Aphrodisiacs   167

10: Awakening to a New Earth   179

Notes   191

Index   201

About the Author   211

Referenced artworks and other images associated
with this text can be found on www.geraldinesbrooks.com.

Acknowledgments

Many beautiful souls generously provided support—tangible and intangible, practical and emotional—during the years it took me to complete this book. It is my honor and pleasure to name them here.

To begin, I offer a very special thank you to my beloved friend Kora Sevier. Kora has been with me every step of my literary journey. She read and patiently re-read the whole and portions of this book and created my lovely website, as well as other related materials. All of this was accomplished with the imagination, aesthetic sensibility, and commitment to beauty that befits the talented artist and designer that she is. But as much as I value Kora's contributions in these areas (and it is a lot), I value even more her unwavering encouragement and companionship along the way to this book's publication.

Two other dear friends read versions of my manuscript, and I give them my heartfelt thanks. Catherine Ellis read an early draft, and her extensive knowledge and understanding of archetypal psychology and the energies of Aphrodite and the Divine Feminine helped greatly in giving shape and focus to my narrative. I am deeply appreciative of Catherine's loving support, not only for this creative endeavor, but also for those that preceded it. Several years and numerous revisions later, Elizabeth Banister kindly read a close-to-final version. Along with other thoughtful reflections, Elizabeth declared it to be "complete." Her gracious reassurance on this point was perfectly timed and helped me transition to the next phase of this book's evolution. Soon afterwards, Susan Madsen offered a review of my text from her perspective as a visual artist and one who values beauty in all things. I thank Susan for her creativity, her enthusiasm for my work, and the wonderful conversations we have had about the subjects I explore in this book.

Thank you also to my two initial publishing consultants: editor Robin Fowler (Speak Memories Publishing) and book designer Linda Parke (Raven Book Design). Robin has a keen eye for detail and an excellent sense of what makes for pleasing narrative flow. Linda generously shared many good ideas and resources as I pursued my publishing goals.

Once I connected with Greenleaf Publishing, I received expert help from various members of their team. Thank you to Maggie Langrick for sharing her knowledge of publishing and welcoming me into the Wonderwell fold, and Dee Kerr for her kindness, humor, and patience with my many questions. I also want to thank Adrianna Hernandez who led the production team, Erin Brown who headed the editorial team, and all those who worked under their careful direction.

I am grateful too for three perceptive and open-hearted men who helped me stay motivated, as well as healthy in mind and body, as I worked to bring this book into being. Robert Sabella and Andrew Smith, astrologers both, provided wise spiritual guidance, including frequent reminders that everything happens according to my soul's good timing. Dr. Mark Cseszko, a gifted healer, attended with warmth and expertise to my physical and mental well-being.

Finally, I want to thank Jehna Chrysler and Adriana Gomes of Hilary Miles Flowers for the artistry they express daily through their work and for keeping me abundantly in roses and other gorgeous blossoms.

NOW, WHILE WE DANCE

Come here to us
gentle Gaiety,
Revelry, Radiance

and you, Muses
with lovely hair

—SAPPHO[1]

Meeting the Goddess
of Love and Beauty

A phrodite calls to us all. Whenever we have a heartfelt response to love and beauty, she is there, inviting us into her sacred realm. It is a realm worth exploring. There is much we can learn from this most alluring of the Greek goddesses about how to be sensuously, creatively, and fully alive.

For those who are new to Aphrodite, this book introduces you to who she is, her most salient myths, her influence on our individual and collective psyches over the ages, and why she is now so important to our spiritual evolution. For those who are already familiar with her, I hope the information I provide here further deepens your knowledge and appreciation of this Goddess and facilitates the integration of her teachings into your life.

Let me set the stage for this examination of Aphrodite and her world by sharing how I came to write about her—as well as Venus, her Roman counterpart—and also provide a glimpse of what I have learned about her transformative powers.

My affinity with Aphrodite-Venus has been lifelong. Perhaps this is because I was born in the sign of Libra, whose ruler is the planet Venus. Or perhaps it is because, as a psychic once told me, I have had previous lifetimes on that planet. Or perhaps it is because something in my individual soul essence responded to Aphrodite's presence from early on in this incarnation. Whatever the case, I know that even as a child, I was drawn to those who seemed to embody the spirit of the Golden Goddess, but I did not have the words then to express the wonder and depth of feeling that her spirit evoked in me. I have the words now, as well as some perspective on how opening to living in the light of Aphrodite and the greater Divine Feminine can direct one's life in wondrous and mysterious ways.

When I reflect on my earliest remembered encounters with Aphrodite, I immediately think of two women who were instrumental in fostering my relationship to her. I consider them both to have been Aphrodite's emissaries on earth, though I strongly doubt either one consciously assumed that role. The first is my late mother, Agnes, who naturally was a major influence in my life. The second is a woman named Ingrid, who I knew only briefly but who made a strong impression on me when I was young. Each of these women was in touch with Aphrodite in a very different way, but my experiences with each of them serve as examples of how the Goddess can present herself in everyday life. Their stories are also emblematic of how we can knowingly or unknowingly live out ancient archetypal scenarios. What I share here about these two women is true, but I have changed a few details to protect their privacy.

I will begin with Ingrid. My best recollection is that I was eleven years old when Ingrid and her husband moved in down the street. Both of them were probably in their late twenties. I may never have known Ingrid's true ancestry, but I always thought of her as Swedish because of her name, coloring, and—to me—refined demeanor. I have distinct memories of Ingrid, but her husband is a nameless and somewhat shadowy figure in my mind. I do remember him being handsome, just as she was beautiful, and that he was away a lot for his job. (I think he was an airline pilot, but that detail may be just my memory's romantic embellishment.) In our middle-class suburban neighborhood, hitherto populated by families and a few retired couples, Ingrid and her husband landed like glamorous aliens.

As I recall, Ingrid did not work outside the home, and I imagine now that she was likely bored, which allowed her the space and inclination to spend time with me, her eager protégée. She would invite me over, and we would talk—maybe about what was happening with the people around us, definitely about clothes and makeup. I liked to watch her get ready to go out, and one time, she gave me a gold tube of pink lipstick that I thought was marvelous. I wish I could remember more of our conversations. I wonder if she ever talked to me about relationships with men considering what happened later that stirred everybody up.

I know Ingrid was a resident in our neighborhood for at

least one summer because I have a clear image of her in her front garden when the sun came out, long blond hair piled on top of her head, wearing a hot pink bikini. This was her usual gardening attire in hot weather, and since the front yard was open to the street, it did not go unnoticed by the neighbors. How could it? She was sensual Aphrodite incarnate. The men and boys were transfixed but tried not to show it, while the women—who responded either with amusement or annoyance depending on their temperament—attempted to quell the curiosity of their children toward this new and powerful phenomenon. And they probably prayed for cold weather.

At about the same time, a single man moved into the house directly opposite Ingrid's. That bachelor, another exotic arrival on our street, was a good-looking, similarly aged redhead by the name of Jack. The next chapter in the story then wrote itself. Jack noticed Ingrid and Ingrid noticed Jack. Aphrodite loves intensely, and she does not care if she incites trouble along the way. Soon I was overhearing whispered gossip about an affair between the two and my wide-eyed young self found it all fascinating.

It was no surprise that the situation quickly got messy. I heard it ended with Ingrid's husband discovering the liaison and putting a stop to it. Ingrid and her husband then moved to another neighborhood. Several years later, Ingrid contacted me and asked if I would babysit their little girl, which I did a few times. I do not know if Ingrid was happy in her marriage, but as far as I could tell, she seemed pleased and proud to be a mother. And I was glad to see that she was still beautiful and still got dressed up to go out. Aphrodite had remained with her but perhaps now shared space with Leto, the Greek Goddess of Motherhood.

The second and even greater—albeit more subtle—influence on my understanding of how Aphrodite may show herself was my mother, Agnes. If I conjure again the image of a curvaceous and provocative Ingrid in her garden, then turn my mind's eye to the other side of the street, I see my mother in our front yard, her hands in the soil, tending an impressive rock garden. In the backyard was an equally impressive vegetable garden, large raspberry and strawberry patches, and two areas of multicolored rose bushes. Roses are Aphrodite's signature flower, though I would be surprised if my mother knew that.

Notably, in none of my memories of my mother gardening is she wearing a bikini. She was a practical woman, and her gardening outfits reflected that practicality. I remember her fondly in a common pose: well-worn cropped cotton pants, a sleeveless shirt, a red bandana on her head, legs apart, and arms akimbo as she surveyed the garden and took stock of what needed doing next.

In her own way, my mother had embraced Aphrodite's gift of bringing forth fruitfulness from the earth. Anyone who ate at our table benefitted from her garden's bounty. She regularly served homegrown vegetables and fruit (fresh and preserved) and, in all seasons, decorated the house with flowers and plant cuttings. I delighted in how every year she would arrange roses on top of my birthday cake. That annual floral ornamentation was a small but sweet indication of Aphrodite's presence.

My mother did not care much for fashion, but she appreciated color in her clothes as in all other things. She was beautiful in her own right and presented herself to the world with little artifice, though she was one of those women who never left the house without red lipstick.

As the Fates would have it, my mother married a man whose life evidenced the influence of Aphrodite's husband, Hephaestus, the Greek God of the Forge. Like Hephaestus, my father was a craftsman. He worked mainly with wood, but he knew how to do metalwork too, and ended up teaching both during his career. Also, Hephaestus was lame due to violence inflicted after his birth by his mother, Hera (Goddess of Marriage). Sadly, my father suffered a similar injury, though from a very different cause—a car accident in his thirties that left him with a permanent painful limp.

It can be astonishing to see how mythological narratives play themselves out in people's lives, though one must not be too literal with such interpretations. For instance, Aphrodite takes for granted the supremacy of love over social conventions like marriage. In the case of my parents, I have no reason to believe that their lives mirrored the many complexities of Aphrodite's relationships.

So, what did I learn about Aphrodite, love, and beauty from these two women?

From Ingrid, I learned that it was important to attend to one's body and to celebrate one's feminine beauty. I learned about the power of that beauty to claim the attention of men and women and that women do not always respond positively to seeing it in another. And I learned that physical beauty, especially when coupled with Aphrodite's drive to honor freedom and autonomy, as well as her valuing of the sensually erotic, can be highly disruptive to the status quo.

From my mother, I learned that having love and beauty as guiding principles can enrich one's life and be a solace when times are hard. She may never have articulated those sentiments, but it is what I understood from watching the way she lived. She tended to show her love in tangible ways, such as by providing those she cared for with a stable home and good nourishing food. As to beauty, my mother did not flaunt her attractiveness like Ingrid. She was much too modest and restrained for that. Rather, she cultivated and honored beauty in her own manner. Her abundant garden, the rose-topped cakes, and her ever-present red lipstick are testaments to that.

My life has not taken the shape of either my mother's or Ingrid's. Like my mother, I am practical in many ways, but not nearly as much as she was. Also, she had a marriage of many decades and bore two children. Neither has been the case for me. My life generally has not been as traditional as hers. But I have inherited, through ancestry or observation, my mother's independent spirit, her pleasure in sharing food and showing hospitality to others, and her love of color and flowers.

Like Ingrid, I take good care of my body and my health, I cultivate my own sense of beauty, and I love dressing up and being appreciated for it. I am, however, not as brazen in my physical display as Ingrid was, and I am very loyal to those I love. That is not to say that I have not been involved in some challenging romantic relationships. I have. But I have come to accept those challenges as a consequence of devotion and acquiescence to the directives of my inner Aphrodite.

In addition to those formative experiences with my mother and Ingrid, there were other important influences in my life that nurtured my interest in Aphrodite and associated mythological figures. From early on I was attracted to reading fairy tales, myths, and legends from many countries. I do not remember ever focusing specifically on Aphrodite or Venus during my school-age years, but I would no doubt have come across their stories. I look back now on all those hours I spent reading about the goddesses, gods, and other invisible forces that can affect us, and I recognize how that time created a psychological and spiritual foundation for later life choices.

I followed my early immersion in mythology with undergraduate studies in art history and literature and then graduate studies in counseling psychology, with a particular interest in the works of psychologist Carl Jung and his followers. My Jungian explorations, especially Jung's discussions of archetypes, led me to revisit the myths and stories that had enchanted me so many years before.

During the decades I devoted to that research, I also attended to developing my spirituality and was increasingly drawn to experiences of the Divine Feminine. Aphrodite then began to call to me through dreams and waking inclinations and, gradually but insistently, made her presence known in my consciousness. As she did so, she guided not only the pursuits of my mind but also the pursuits of my heart. She still does.

As I explain in the following chapter, our current chaotic and violent world is desperately in need of the balancing force of Divine Feminine energy. Aphrodite's gifts of love and beauty are vital aspects of that essential energy. Love and beauty, consciously experienced and expressed, carry the power to elevate and heal us, both individually and collectively. It is time for us all to respond to Aphrodite's invitation and share her life-affirming gifts with the world.

May this book awaken or strengthen in you a personal relationship with Aphrodite and the positive transformative energy she represents. As you read these pages, if you allow your mind and heart to open to this beloved Goddess, you too may come to value and honor her as I do.

This is her promise and her blessing:

> She is feminine nature in all its glory.
> She is a celebration of love and life.
> She can make your life complicated.
> She can make your life beautiful.
> Her divine presence will change you if you let it.
>
> —GERALDINE S. BROOKS

Chapter 1

Awakening to Aphrodite in Our Wounded World

Civilized life, you know, is based on a huge number of illusions
in which we collaborate willingly. The trouble is we forget after
a while that they are illusions, and we are deeply shocked
when reality is torn down around us.

—J. G. BALLARD[1]

There is no going back. Nor should we want to. Though some will continue to long for the familiar structures and apparent stability of earlier times, what they may not yet or perhaps ever realize is that amidst the immense turmoil and strife of recent years, our world is being irrevocably altered for the good. The political, economic, social, and spiritual shifts we are experiencing are profound and wide-ranging, and they will benefit us all in the years to come.

For the present though, and likely for the near and indeterminate future, we will need to navigate between two interconnected but divergent realities. On the one hand, we are living through a worldwide collapse of corrupt and inhumane oligarchies, institutions, and systems that have long controlled and exploited earth's diverse resources and life forms, including humans. The process of that collapse is chaotic, often violent, and our recovery from it will take considerable time. On the other hand, we are in the midst of a powerful transformation in collective consciousness. It is the Great Awakening and it has the power to radically change our personal and shared reality. Both phenomena are vitally important to the development of humanity and the earth and will unquestionably define our era.

As increasing numbers of people are becoming aware of the magnitude of the changes taking place and are embracing the concept of a Great Awakening, they are expressing excitement as well as gratitude for being alive to be a part of it. This is even though they may be adversely affected by the changes underway. Significant transformation of any type is never uniformly pleasant.

At the same time, many others are far from enthusiastic about these changes or their attendant revelations. Over the past several years, we have all witnessed terrible and frightening events take place, internationally if not locally. And it is understandably shocking, painful, and confusing to realize that what one has accepted as truths about the world, including the trustworthiness of lauded individuals, groups, and organizations, or even the basic history and science most of us have been taught—indeed, the very foundational structures and central organizing principles of our civilization—now need full-scale revision.

Some will experience the dissolution of their cherished beliefs about reality and their accustomed way of life as traumatic and will not be able to integrate what is happening around them without considerable difficulty, if at all. But those who are willing to welcome the idea that we are undergoing no less than a universal transformation in consciousness have an opportunity to experience a new kind of freedom: liberation from dark internal and external forces that have limited our personal and shared perceptions of the world and our power to live fully as divine sovereign beings. We are now being invited to imagine and create lives that can be truly safe and secure, meaningful and purposeful, and in which life-sustaining resources, joy, and love are abundant.

In order for most of us to reach such a blessed state, however, healing is necessary. The changes afoot may ultimately be positive, but they are still deeply disturbing. It is hard to let go of established paradigms of "truth" and "reality" that have helped us make sense of the world. But if those paradigms have been based on lies and manipulation, letting go of them is exactly what we need to do. Any limiting attitudinal and behavioral patterns we have adopted in order to live in accordance with them need identification, emotional processing, and, ultimately, transcendence. Healing from trauma is not just about understanding the impact of wounding experiences but also about consciously choosing to move forward toward something better.

THE DIVINE FEMININE

On a spiritual level, a major contributor to the chaos, confusion, and fear we have experienced is our culture's long-standing disconnection from the Divine Feminine, that is, the positive energy of the feminine in the universe. ("Energy" in this context is used to designate the qualities of a particular level of consciousness. It can also be understood as a set of physical frequencies related to that level of consciousness.)

Divine or Sacred Feminine energy is an integral part of both the cosmos and every individual. It is energy that is connected to nature, fertility, and the cycles of life and death, and it is manifested in humans as a positive force that is loving, nurturing, fluid, creative, intuitive, and grounded in the body. Gentleness, compassion, and patience are also associated with the Divine Feminine, but never weakness; Divine Feminine energy can be fierce when the sanctity of truth, life, and Mother Earth are threatened. Disconnection from the Divine Feminine can be seen in qualities and experiences linked with negative feminine energy, such as passivity, victimhood, emotional manipulation, and separation from nature and one's body.

[The Feminine Divine] is so bright and glorious that
you cannot look at her face or her garments for the
splendor with which she shines. For she is terrible with
the terror of the avenging lightening, and gentle with
the goodness of the bright sun; and both her terror and
her gentleness are incomprehensible to humans . . . But

she is with everyone and in everyone, and so beautiful
is her secret that no person can know the sweetness
with which she sustains people, and spares them in
inscrutable mercy.

—SAINT HILDEGARD OF BINGEN, *Scivias*

———————

The world we have been living in has dishonored Divine
Feminine energy for thousands of years. The proof is our
history of violence in its many manifestations; our highly
dysfunctional, unequal, and regimented social order; and the
resultant stress, pain, and suffering we have all experienced to
varying degrees.

A majority of the established systems we have been interacting with (governmental, educational, medical, religious, and
mass media) have been pervaded by negative masculine energy.
This energy is characterized by an exaggerated emphasis on
control, dominance, glorification of conflict, emotional sup-
pression, and a lack of empathy. In contrast, Divine Masculine
energy is equated with strength, courage, protectiveness, logic,
and action, among other positive characteristics.

Many of our established systems, contrary to their stated
goals, have propagated ignorance, fear, and passivity in the
populace, whether well-intentioned individuals working within
those systems have meant to foster such outcomes or not. In
addition, almost everyone living in the West has been exposed,
usually daily and over many years, to messages from authority
figures, celebrities, and influencers of various types promoting

the views that we are inherently unworthy and flawed (indeed, born into "sin" according to traditional Christian doctrine); we have little significance or agency in the world as "ordinary" citizens; and life is about the acquisition of wealth and status, competition for scarce resources, struggle, and the endurance of suffering. Furthermore, much programming on television and other mainstream media advocates that we would do best to acquiesce our decision-making power to societally chosen role models and enforcers.

A sad result of our exposure to these repetitive messages is that the majority of people spend a disproportionate amount of time and energy working in ways that are mentally and physically debilitating in order to stay afloat financially and then consume products and services that are designed to distract us or promise to make our lives better but usually do not—or at least not with any permanence. That all-too-common state of being has led to a widespread experience of disconnection from nature, a lack of awareness of true health and healing practices, and ignorance of who we really are: multidimensional sovereign beings with tremendous physical, mental, and spiritual capabilities.

The fact that we are now witnessing broadscale physical and emotional health problems in many countries of the world, including serious depression and anxiety, is not at all surprising. Those disorders make sense if one feels powerless to change the conditions of one's life and if the detrimental effects of living, sporadically or permanently, in physical or psychological survival mode do not diminish. Such an existence is antithetical to both Divine Feminine and Divine Masculine consciousness.

It is important to recognize that the energy of the Divine Feminine is universal and not gender specific. Divine Feminine energy does not belong solely to women, just as Divine Masculine energy does not belong solely to men. And neither energy is superior to nor should supersede the other. As more and more people now aspire to grow in consciousness, they are recognizing the value of connecting to both Divine energies. To reach spiritual maturity, these two energies need to be balanced and working in harmony. When this is achieved (no small feat), the next spiritual challenge is to unify these energies within ourselves and then, ultimately, transcend their inherent duality so that we may become truly integrated Divine Humans.

APHRODITE

In the following chapters, I discuss particular aspects of the Divine Feminine, especially as represented by the Greek Goddess Aphrodite. I address ways in which long-standing devaluations of the characteristics and principles associated with this Goddess have contributed to the creation of unhealthy and unbalanced societies and fostered a limited understanding of our true potential as humans. I examine who Aphrodite was mythologically and how she continues to function as a potent archetype in human psychology, the nature of her transformative powers in the domains of love and beauty, and what Aphrodite's energy brings to our understanding of embodied love and the potential sanctity of sex. I also explore what beauty is and what it is not, why we so often have trouble accessing the beauty around us, how to better engage our senses in the service of love and beauty, the enlightened use of aphrodisiacs, and finally, how awakening Aphrodite in our lives can facilitate positive personal and collective change.

Throughout the text, I give examples of personal reflections and practices that help facilitate emotional, psychological, and spiritual growth and healing through the honoring of Aphrodite. Both men and women will benefit from understanding how embodiment of her teachings can help them live in balanced, authentic, heart-centered, and joyful ways. The more we all can awaken to a fully conscious experience of Aphrodite and the greater Divine Feminine, the better we will be able to heal ourselves and our world and together create a new and beautiful earth for everyone.

> If we start with the world as something beautiful, we would want to keep it around. That's the simplest answer to the problem of the world. . . . Once we really appreciate beauty, we can fall in love with the world. Not just love it, but fall in love with it. And you only fall in love with it if you're aesthetically alive to it.
>
> —JAMES HILLMAN, *"The Practice of Beauty"*

A few things to consider while reading . . .

About "myth": The word comes from the Greek term *mythos*,

which can mean "word," "tale," or "true narrative." These alternative meanings are important to keep in mind because any myth might be understood on three levels. First, a myth reflects in symbolic form archetypal or universal experiences from our real lives (such as birth, death, and love). Second, it may reference actual historical events or parts of them. Third, a myth is a fictional story that one should not take at face value. As such, myths could have been and undoubtedly were modified and reinterpreted over time according to changes in the collective's conscious and unconscious needs and desires. For this reason, there exist multiple versions and interpretations of the ancient myths I discuss. In each case, I have tried to present the version that is currently the best-known, but one could easily find other renditions with many different details.

Also, while research into mythology can be fascinating, to spend much time scrutinizing the "accuracy" of one mythical account over another is to miss the point if what you are seeking is the psychological and spiritual truths at their heart. The real purpose of myths is to reveal the timeless underlying patterns of human existence. Knowledge of these patterns can give meaning to our lives and also help guide our behavior. In the words of comparative religion scholar Karen Armstrong:

> Correctly understood, mythology puts us in the correct spiritual or psychological posture for right action, in this world or the next. . . . All mythology speaks of another plane that exists alongside our own world, and that in some sense supports it. Belief in this invisible

but more powerful reality, sometimes called the world of the gods, is a basic theme ... It is only by participating in this divine life that mortal, fragile human beings fulfil their potential. . . . [Myths told people] how the gods behaved, not out of idle curiosity or because these tales were entertaining, but to enable men and women to imitate these powerful beings and experience divinity themselves.[2]

What is most important, then, in assessing a myth's current value is not whether it reflects truth in a factual sense but to what degree it has remained true psychologically and spiritually and whether it has retained the power to influence our experience and affect us positively. Not all myths last, but there is no doubt that the figure of Aphrodite and the myths about her continue to have relevance for us. The Goddess in her many forms would not still be so prominent in our psyches if that were not the case. But we must never forget that Aphrodite is an archetypal being, not a human one, meaning that she is a primordial, universal, and timeless image and not a historical personage.

As such, despite the specificity of her Grecian birth story, she has never been and never will be bound to time or place or restricted by human limitations. Furthermore, some galactic historians believe that what we now think of as the goddesses and gods from ancient times are actually our symbolic representations of beings from other planets or dimensions who first visited Earth many millennia ago and who, through their interventions, shaped our history and perceptions of who and what we really are, and continue to do so.

In any case, because we cannot precisely pin down the origin or veracity of any mythological narrative, to gain the fullest appreciation of a figure like Aphrodite, it is best to set aside reliance on facts, logic, and reason as the principal means of understanding. A more rewarding approach is to concentrate on opening emotionally to the richness and mystery of this Goddess's divine essence, which shines through all the enduring stories about her.

Another concept to consider is history. The term "apocalypse" is now commonly used to refer to either the final battle between earthly and heavenly forces leading to the end of the world (as prophesized in the Bible's book of Revelation) or, more generally, to any event deemed a widespread disaster. However, the original meaning of the term, derived from the Greek, is that of a "revealing" or an "unveiling" of what has been hidden. That is surely what we have been experiencing over recent decades as so many disturbing truths have come to light about all aspects of our world. There is good reason to believe we have been systematically lied to on multiple fronts, including our history—that is, not only about what events happened when, where, and to whom, but about our very origin and development as a species.

I am not a historian, galactic or otherwise, and cannot personally vouch for the historical data I will present in these pages. I can say that I have done my best to provide credible information based on sources considered reputable at the time of this writing. We may find in the future that much if not most (or even all?) of this information is wrong. The mathematician Anatoly Fomenko, one of the founders of the "New Chronology" movement, is only one of many researchers who has challenged the validity of the commonly accepted world civilizational timeline. Fomenko and his colleagues, for example, have contended that recorded history before the seventeenth century (including the history of ancient Egypt, Greece, and Rome) is generally unreliable and was probably fabricated.[3]

Others have gone further and asserted that much or most of what we believe about world history up to the present day (including major world events) may be inaccurate. Those possibilities notwithstanding, the timelines and "facts" I share, whatever their relative accuracy, do not negate the idea that Aphrodite, like her associate goddesses and gods, has been present as a compelling archetypal force in many cultures for a very long time.

Finally, about Sappho, whose poems enfold the main text of this book: Sappho was (or considering the earlier caveat, is said to be) a late sixth to early fifth century BCE lyric poet who was born and lived on the Greek island of Lesbos. She has been admired through the ages for the beauty and sensitivity she brought to bear on the content of her writings, as well as her personally revealing and engaging style. She is also known for leading a *thiasos*, a community of young women who were dedicated to cultivating the knowledge and arts of the Muses and the worship of Aphrodite.

Frequent themes in Sappho's poetry are romantic passion,

wedding songs, invocations to particular gods and goddesses, and the sensuous details of rituals devoted to them—especially those devoted to Aphrodite, the divine muse who inspired and guided Sappho and her followers and who continues to inspire and guide many people to this day. Unfortunately, because her poems were written on papyrus scrolls that were destroyed or deteriorated over time, only fragments of most of her work remain.

Here is a lovely sample of Sappho's poetry to begin our exploration into the abiding value of Aphrodite, beloved Goddess of Love and Beauty. May the light of the Divine Feminine guide us on our way.

STANDING BY MY BED

In gold sandals
Dawn that very
moment awoke me

—SAPPHO[4]

Chapter 2

Who Is Aphrodite?

Muse, tell me the works of golden-throned Aphrodite,
Kypris, who stirs up sweet longing in gods
and subdues the tribes of mortal men,
winged birds and all the beasts,
as many things as the land and the sea nurture.
The works of Aphrodite of beautiful garlands concern all.

—HOMER, "Homeric Hymn to Aphrodite"

In the ancient Greek pantheon, each god or goddess was considered to have dominion over one or more realms that correspond to areas of importance for humans. Aphrodite was the Olympian Goddess of Love and Beauty. As noted earlier, she was—and is—a universal and timeless archetype who represents particular aspects of the feminine psyche (conscious and unconscious). Additional aspects of the feminine are represented by other goddesses from the same mythic lineage, including Athena, Goddess of Wisdom and Crafts;

Artemis, Goddess of the Hunt; Hera, Goddess of Marriage; and Demeter, Goddess of the Harvest.

Aspects of the masculine psyche are similarly represented by gods from that lineage, such as Zeus, God of the Sky and Thunder and Ruler of the Olympians; Poseidon, God of the Sea; Apollo, God of the Sun; and Hermes, Messenger of the Gods. All these deities are inherited archetypes that are part of the human psyche. That is, they live in the unconscious of each one of us though we might experience the "presence" and influence of any one of them to varying degrees throughout our lives.

Also, the stories of these deities, while they are writ large compared to those of mortals, are rooted in familiar human experiences. Attending to these ancient stories and noticing which narratives and figures we most relate to at any given time can help us better understand ourselves and others, especially when we feel compelled to act in ways that are out of our usual character. In such situations, our thoughts, feelings, and behaviors may be driven by archetypal energies acting in and through us. To experience the power of the goddesses and gods at work in that way can be disorienting, even disturbing, but it can also be enlivening when it connects us to a greater sense of mystery, meaning, and purpose in our lives.

Aphrodite, like the other deities listed earlier, is a specifically Greek goddess, but her name and influence are not limited to the country of her birth. Even in other cultures that have claimed their own Goddess of Love and Beauty, Aphrodite can be considered present and active because she is a manifestation of the same universal energetic force. That force just varies in name and details in different places and eras. For example, Hathor in Egypt, Freya in the Norse Lands (Scandinavia), and Sri Lakshmi in India. I have chosen to focus on Aphrodite not only because she is a goddess of personal interest to me but because she is such a well-known and well-loved—and therefore psychologically and spiritually powerful—representation of the forces of love and beauty throughout the Western world.

Of course, we also have a strong affiliation in the West with Venus, the ancient Roman Goddess of Love. Venus is the goddess most closely associated with Aphrodite, and the Goddess of Love is often referred to as Venus-Aphrodite or Aphrodite-Venus. Early records suggest, however, that the emergence of Aphrodite in the collective psyche of ancient Greece preceded that of Venus in the Roman Empire. Venus then became identified with the preexisting archetype of Aphrodite rather than the other way around.

In addition to being the designation of a goddess, Venus is the name of the planet that comes closest to the Earth in its orbit. Appropriately, the planet Venus, also known as the Morning Star and Evening Star, is said by astrologers to influence how one relates to love and beauty, as well as money. In what follows, I occasionally use the names of Aphrodite and Venus interchangeably. Writers, artists, and scholars from different historical and cultural backgrounds have favored the use of one name and image over the other, but both Aphrodite and Venus refer to essentially the same archetype.

Looking back further into antiquity, we can see that Aphrodite evolved from even more ancient goddesses such as Isis in Egypt, Astarte in the ancient Near East, Inanna in Sumer, and Ishtar in Mesopotamia, but the names of these and other preexisting goddesses, with the possible exception of Isis, do not have as much resonance as Aphrodite and Venus in the general consciousness of contemporary Western society. Still, it is important to acknowledge the powerful lineage that led to the emergence of Aphrodite-Venus and her sister goddesses in order to fully understand their role and influence in our lives.

Long before the Greeks and the Romans established their gods and goddesses, the feminine force of the Great Goddess was understood to be the source of life and death and the great mystery of existence. Her title varied—she was sometimes referred to as the Great Mother Goddess, the Cosmic Mother, the Divine Mother, or simply the Goddess—and she took many forms around the world but was consistently envisioned as having control over all aspects of a culture. The mythologist Joseph Campbell emphasized this point: "People often think of the Goddess as a fertility deity only. Not at all—she is the muse. She is the inspirer of poetry. She is the inspirer of the spirit. So, she has three functions: one, to give us life; two, to be the one who receives us in death; and three, to inspire our spiritual poetic realization."[1]

Historians say that the Greek myths we know today may

have originated in stories told by Minoan and Mycenaean bards from as early as 1800 BCE (or even 3000 BCE, according to some sources). This was centuries before Homer penned the *Illiad* and the *Odyssey*, epic poems from c. 800 BCE, which contain the most popular versions of those myths. It is not clear when, in the evolutionary process of the Greek myths, different facets of the Great Goddess's power began to be specified and associated with separate goddesses and gods. But it is evident that as the culture of ancient Greece (also known as the Hellenic period) took shape, not only did the Great Goddess lose much of her encompassing spiritual authority, but the new distinct goddesses also became subordinate in stature to new distinct male gods, including a male supreme god in the form of Zeus.

Anthropologist Jane Ellen Harrison is credited with being one of the first scholars to recognize that pre-Hellenic mythology was dominated by a matricentric earth spirit. She contended that a supreme male deity did not emerge in Greek culture until about 2500 BCE, following many thousands of years of Goddess-centered worship.[2] That development marked a profound shift in the religious attitude of those ancient peoples and contributed to a persistent overvaluation of the masculine principle at the expense of the feminine principle.

Nevertheless, each distinct goddess remained—and remains—connected through her genesis to the Great Goddess. In Aphrodite's case, although she is considered to be one of the later additions to the Greek pantheon (possibly dating from as late as c. 800 BCE), she still carries the primordial energies of nature, fecundity, and rebirth in her association with love, and the energy of "our spiritual poetic realization,"[3] as Campbell phrased it, in her association with beauty. These energies were interpreted broadly in ancient times and were understood to extend to such diverse realms as sailing (Aphrodite had influence over the sea), civic order, and even the military and war—any area of life where harmony and union might be desired. Consequently, a single city might build multiple shrines to Aphrodite, each dedicated to a different aspect of her authority.[4] This declaration by Aphrodite, presented by the dramatist Aeschylus (525–455 BCE), speaks to her wide-ranging powers:

> I am the Goddess Cypria, mighty among people.
> They honour me by many names.
> From the tides of Pontus to the Pillars of Atlas
> These lands are mine to rule.
> To those who acknowledge my power,
> I give honours and rewards.
> But those who dare to defy me,
> I shall swing them by their heels.
> For how can I be joyous in my heart,
> If I am not honoured by my people?[5]

Later, Plato in his *Symposium* (c. 385–370 BCE) differentiated between Aphrodite's powers in the domain of love by giving her two titles: Aphrodite Urania (daughter of the god Uranus) and Aphrodite Pandemos (meaning "common to all the people"). Aphrodite Urania equated the Goddess with spiritual or celestial love, while Aphrodite Pandemos equated her with earthly non-spiritual love, which extended to civic and interpersonal harmony. As Aphrodite Pandemos, she was also linked to Peitho, the Goddess of Charming Speech and Persuasion, who in some myths was named as her companion or attendant and who could be prayed to for assistance in seduction. Philosophers, writers, and artists during and after Plato's time adopted these two titles for Aphrodite and employed them in art and literature over many centuries.

In the modern era, however, not only is it rare to see a distinction made between Aphrodite Urania and Aphrodite Pandemos but the Goddess has often been reduced simply to the role of the "sexy one" among the Greek deities. One only has to do an internet search for images of Aphrodite to see how she is now frequently portrayed. Alongside illustrations of ancient and modern artworks with her likeness are many cute and coy cartoonish figures, as well as photos of real women, some ethereal in their presentation, others sexually provocative. Much of this imaging is highly reductive and does Aphrodite's archetypal power a grave disservice. She remains a force to be reckoned with, as we shall see. At the same time, the vast number and types of representations of the Goddess, from thousands of years old marble statuary to contemporary plastic figurines, attest to her lasting relevance.

The great and amorous sky curved over the earth
and lay upon her as a pure lover.
The rain, the humid flux, descending from heaven
for both man and animal, for both thick and strong,
germinated the wheat, swelled the furrows with fecund mud
and brought forth the buds in the orchards.
And it is I who empowered these moist espousals,
I, the great Aphrodite.

—AESCHYLUS, _The Danaides_

THE MYTHS OF APHRODITE

Numerous versions of Aphrodite's origin story have appeared over the centuries, but all establish her associations with the fruitfulness of nature. The myth that is most familiar to us in modern times is based on the writings of the ancient Greek poet Hesiod (c. 750–650 BCE), who located her birth near Paphos on the island of Cyprus. (Hesiod's contemporary, the poet Homer, similarly identified Aphrodite as "the lady of Kypros.") According to Hesiod, as well as to many subsequent iterations of his story, Aphrodite's parents were Uranus (or Ouranos), the primordial God of the Sky or Heaven, and Dione, an Oceanid nymph. However, in some versions, Aphrodite's mother was identified as Gaia, another primordial deity and vastly more powerful than an Oceanid nymph. (Consistent with the complexities of mythological genealogy, Uranus was Gaia's first child, whom she later married.)

The Greeks believed that before time began, the universe was in a state of Chaos. Gaia was the first deity to emerge from Chaos at the beginning of time, and she became the mother of life on Earth. The identification of Gaia as our original mother has left an indelible mark on our collective psyche, and to this day, we commonly refer to the Earth by her name or as Mother Earth.

Also, although Gaia is primarily associated with the land (terra), as the primeval mother of *all* planetary life, she can be considered the mother of the sea and other earthly waters as well. This appellation is appropriate because the sea and water are understood to be the ultimate source and supporter of all life and are almost universally considered feminine elements. Later, as the number of goddesses and gods increased over time, several of Gaia's descendants were identified as ruling over different types and qualities of water, such as rivers.

Furthermore, the identification of Gaia as the mother of Aphrodite (rather than the nymph Dione) significantly elevates the circumstances of Aphrodite's birth. If Gaia is her mother, then Aphrodite is the daughter of a union between two great primordial deities: Gaia, the original Goddess of the Earth, and Uranus, the original God of the Sky. This underscores her symbolic import as an especially powerful manifestation of Divine Feminine energy.

To return to Hesiod's narrative: In order to rescue his mother from Uranus's oppressive lust, their youngest son, Cronus, Ruler of Time, castrated his father and threw his genitals into the sea. Uranus's genitals gradually floated toward Cyprus, and as they did so, a white foam (*aphros*) gathered around them. This foam gave rise to Aphrodite as a beautiful young woman who rode to the Cyprian shore on a scallop shell. This is why Aphrodite is referred to as "foam-born." The city of Paphos grew in the place where she landed, and it was there that Aphrodite would return each spring to bathe in the sea and renew herself. This is a key detail if we consider the sea to be an expression of Gaia, the Great Mother, and her regenerative power.

Scholar Charlene Spretnak presented an evocative narrative of Aphrodite's emergence into the world and the influence of her enduring presence:

> Life was young and frail when Aphrodite arose with the breadth of renewal. Borne by gentle winds on the eastern sea, she alighted on the island of Cyprus. So graceful and alluring was the Goddess that the Seasons rushed to meet her, imploring her always to stay. Aphrodite smiled. Her stay would be never-ending, her work never complete. She crossed the pebbled beach and wandered over the hills and plains, seeking out all living creatures. Magically she touched them with desire and sent them off in joyous pairs. She blessed the females' wombs, guarded them as they grew, and warded off love's pains at birth. Everywhere, Aphrodite drew forth the hidden promise of life. Every day she kissed the earth with morning dew. The wanderings of the Goddess carried her far, yet each spring she returned with her doves to Cyprus for her sacred bath at

Paphos. There she was attended by her Graces: Flowering, Growth, Beauty, Joy, and Radiance. They crowned her with myrtle and laid a path of rose petals at her feet. Aphrodite walked into the sea, into the pulsing moon rhythms of the tide. When she emerged with her spirit renewed, spring blossomed fully and all beings felt her joy. Through seasons, years, eras, Aphrodite's mysteries remain inviolable, for she alone understands that love begets life.[6]

SYMBOLS OF APHRODITE

In ancient Greece, Aphrodite, like every deity, was associated with certain easily recognizable symbols that referenced her essence and life story. These symbols were commonly included in rituals of worship and artwork, as well as carried as talismans, worn as jewelry, and incorporated into the decoration of homes to invite the Goddess's blessings and protection. Some of the symbols associated with Aphrodite were drawn from cultures even older than that of Greece, most notably Mesopotamia and the Near East, where Inanna/Ishtar was worshipped.

One of Aphrodite's most potent symbols was the golden girdle made for her as a wedding gift by her husband Hephaestus, God of the Forge. Its appearance is open to interpretation but might best be thought of as an ornamented breastpiece or bra. Her girdle had the magical power to enhance—or in Aphrodite's case, to further enhance—the wearer's beauty and desirability. Its powers were most famously put to use by Aphrodite (to her husband Hephaestus's dismay) in her adulterous affair with Ares and by Hera, who borrowed the girdle to win back the attention of her husband, Zeus.

continued

Many of the ancient symbols of Aphrodite continue to hold meaning for us. They still appear in depictions of the Goddess and have become easily identifiable symbols of love and beauty more generally. Appropriately, most of them relate to some aspect of nature.

- Season—Spring
- Day—the Fourth of the Month (specifically the fourth day following the New Moon based on the Athenian calendar)
- Sea Elements—Shells (especially Scallop Shells), Pearls
- Minerals—Rose Quartz, Lapis Lazuli, Jade
- Metals—Gold, Copper
- Planet—Venus (the Morning and Evening Star)
- Birds—Doves, Sparrows, Swans, Geese, Ducks
- Flowers—Roses, Red Anemones, Myrtle
- Fruits—Apples (especially Red or Golden), Quince, Pomegranates
- Colors—Pink, Red, Light Green (Sea-Foam Green), Light Blue
- Objects—Mirrors
- Transport—For the sky, a Golden, Jewel-Encrusted Chariot pulled by Doves or Swans; For the sea, a Shell Chariot pulled by Mermen

The Greek myths relate tales of Aphrodite's many romantic encounters with gods and mortals, as well as a sea nymph. These include four other Olympian deities: Ares, God of War (their relationship is described shortly); Hermes, Messenger of the

Gods, with whom she bore a son, the bisexual Hermaphroditos; Poseidon, God of the Sea, with whom she had two daughters, Rhodos and Herophilos; and Dionysus, God of Wine, with whom she had an ugly son, Priapos (Hera's punishment for Aphrodite's promiscuity), and possibly another daughter, Peitho. (Peitho's parentage is uncertain.) Aphrodite was also married to the Olympian Hephaestus, the lame God of the Forge, though their relationship is not considered one of her true romances.

Aphrodite's relationship with Ares was passionate and long-standing and was the most committed affair among the Olympians. Aphrodite's amorous disposition and feminine sensibility were well matched by Ares's similarly intense but more earthy masculine sensuality. It is variously said that Aphrodite and Ares had between three and nine children; the number depends on the mythological source consulted, though most agree there were at least four. The children usually named are Harmonia, Goddess of Harmony; Phobos, God of Fear; Deimos, God of Terror; and Eros, God of Love.

There is debate, however, as to whether or not Eros was truly the son of Aphrodite and Ares (Hermes has also been named as his father) or if he was Aphrodite's son but fatherless (this could harken back to the ability of the Great Goddess to give birth parthenogenetically) or if he was, as Hesiod wrote, one of the primordial gods. If Eros was primordial, he would have existed before the Olympians and even the earlier Titans. Some sources say this must be the case; otherwise, how could the gods and goddesses from those eras have fallen in love with each other? I explore Eros's connection to Aphrodite more fully in Chapter 5.

Regarding Aphrodite's relationships with mortals, one of the most notable was the love affair she had with Anchises, a member of the royal family of Troy. Aphrodite desired Anchises and seduced him by pretending to be a Phrygian princess. Here is an excerpt from the "Homeric Hymn to Aphrodite" (note that in Homer's writings, Zeus, the Olympian God of the Sky and Thunder, was named as Aphrodite's father):

> . . . She stood before him, the daughter of Zeus,
> Aphrodite, like an unsubdued virgin in size and looks,
> lest he discern her with his eyes and be afraid.
> Anchises, seeing her, pondered in wonderment
> over her looks and size and glittering clothes.
> She was clothed in a dress more gleaming than bright fire. Like
> the moon, it shimmered around her soft breasts, a wonder to
> behold. She wore coiled bracelets and shining earrings,
> and beautiful necklaces were about her tender neck,
> beautiful, golden, glittering.[7]

Their affair was brief but ardent. When Aphrodite revealed to Anchises who she really was, he was shocked and afraid of her power—also, the punishment for a man who slept with an immortal was impotence—but Aphrodite told him he had nothing to fear as long as he did not tell anyone he had slept with a goddess. She also told him that their union would produce a son, Aeneas, who was destined to become the hero of Troy and Rome. However, one day when drunk, Anchises bragged to his friends about Aphrodite's love for him. Betraying a goddess's confidence was a serious transgression, and it led to Zeus crippling Anchises with a thunderbolt.

The most well-known story of Aphrodite's love for a mortal is that of her relationship with Adonis who was the son of King Cinyras of Cyprus (or alternatively, King Theias of Assyria) and his daughter Myrrha. Myrrha's mother (or perhaps father) had proclaimed Myrrha to be more beautiful than Aphrodite. As punishment, the Goddess placed a curse on Myrrha that caused her to trick her father into an incestuous union. When Myrrha's father learned of her deception, he threatened to kill her. The gods (or, in some renditions, Aphrodite herself) took pity and transformed Myrrha into a myrrh tree to save her. Her father found the tree, struck it with his sword, and it cracked open to reveal the infant Adonis.

In one version of the myth, Aphrodite came upon this scene, was immediately smitten by the beautiful boy, and hid him in a coffer, which she entrusted to the care of Persephone, Goddess of the Underworld. But when Persephone opened the coffer, she also fell in love with the child and did not want to return him to Aphrodite.

Another version says that the young adult Adonis, reported to be the most handsome of men, caught Aphrodite's eye while she was playing outside with her son Eros. When one of Eros's arrows accidentally hit her, she fell deeply in love with Adonis, and he with her. In that version, Persephone later observed Aphrodite and Adonis together and she too fell in love with Adonis with some help from another of Eros's arrows.

Whatever the circumstances of their first encounter, the myths stress Aphrodite's immediate love for Adonis and her rivalry with Persephone for his attentions.

Adonis was an avid hunter, and his enthusiasm for that dangerous activity worried Aphrodite. Her fears were realized when he was fatally wounded by a wild boar. (Some accounts say that the boar was a jealous Ares in disguise, others that Artemis had sent the animal to attack Adonis because he had boasted that he was a better hunter than she was.) Aphrodite heard Adonis's anguished cries and rushed to his side, but as she did so, she cut her foot on the thorns of a white rose, and her blood stained it red. Adonis died in her arms, and as Aphrodite wept, her tears united with his blood and became anemone flowers. This is said to be the origin of the association between those two flowers and love. Red roses continue to be a symbol of passionate love and short-lived red anemones a symbol of Aphrodite and Adonis's too-brief love affair.

Aphrodite and Persephone fought fiercely about Adonis after his death, and each begged Zeus to bring him back to life. Zeus finally decreed that he would resurrect Adonis to spend one-third of the year with Persephone in the Underworld, one-third with Aphrodite in the Upperworld, and one-third wherever he liked. To Aphrodite's delight, Adonis chose to spend his discretionary months with her.

The story of Aphrodite and Adonis is one of the most salient elements of the overall myth of Aphrodite. The ancient core of this narrative—the relationship of the Great Mother Goddess to her son—was a major component of many early religions. It is an archetypal narrative of death and resurrection, which among other things, shows the regenerative power of love and the feminine. In Aphrodite's case, the Great Goddess's son is symbolized by the handsome youth Adonis.

This aspect of Aphrodite's myth was of great importance to the Greeks, and a cult and an annual festival called Adonia formed around it. The festival, said to have been initiated by Aphrodite herself, was held by Athenian and Cyprian women in midsummer though there is debate about its exact timing. It commemorated Adonis's death and rebirth as well as Aphrodite's—and by extension, all women's—ability to bestow life. As part of the observances, women would wear wreaths of red anemones and myrtle in their hair, carry pomegranates to represent Persephone, who also mourned his death, and plant "Adonis gardens" of fennel or lettuce (both considered to be aphrodisiac plants) or other quick-growing seeds in shallow pots or terracotta shards on their rooftops. The gardens would come to life only to soon wither and die. The purpose of these temporary gardens was to symbolize the brief flourishing of Adonis's life. They were also used to hold effigies of Adonis, which were carried through the streets in a ritual funeral procession and then either tossed into the sea or buried in order to sprout again.[8]

While Aphrodite had many lovers, Hephaestus was her only husband. Hephaestus was a talented craftsman but typically portrayed as a bit of a buffoon. His marriage to Aphrodite was arranged by Zeus (who, in many accounts, is identified as Hephaestus's father) and was not a love match, at least not for

Aphrodite. She therefore felt no loyalty to him and even passed off her children by Ares to Hephaestus as his own.

Upon discovering Aphrodite and Ares's relationship, Hephaestus set a trap for the two lovers and called upon the other gods and goddesses to witness and judge his wife's infidelity. But the goddesses stayed home and the gods, rather than condemning Aphrodite, were themselves entranced by her, and she went on to have affairs with several of them. Aphrodite and Hephaestus did not have any children together. Instead, their marriage has come to symbolize the joining of beauty and craft.

It has been said that Aphrodite should never have married at all because her true nature is to be autonomous and proud, as well as unambivalent and unselfconscious about her body and her sexuality. Her commitment is to the values of love, beauty, pleasure, and creativity, not rules or social conventions. (Also, unlike many of her sister goddesses, Aphrodite was never raped.) Author Agapi Stassinopoulos captured this aspect of Aphrodite:

> . . . Aphrodite is the quintessential lover, the ultimate seductress who takes endless pleasure in her own physical attributes and in bestowing her gifts upon her lovers. She resists being tamed or tied down to one man but never becomes jaded or hardened by her experiences. Rather, she remains the perpetual virgin lover, giving herself each time, as if it were the first. For her, love is always the answer.[9]

Notably, the meaning of "virgin" has changed considerably over time. We now usually use the term to refer to someone who has not had sex, but *virgo*, the Latin root word of "virgin," had different connotations in the ancient world. At times it was used to signify "strength" or "power"—and so carries the same generative energy as "virility"—and at other times, it signified someone who simply was "unmarried." Subsequent to those usages, "virgin" came to mean a woman who was "one unto herself," that is, a sovereign being who neither belongs to nor is defined by any man and who is free to make her own choices, sexual and otherwise. It is in that sense, as one who is true to her own nature and endowed with the ability to renew herself as she pleases, that Aphrodite is sometimes referred to as a Virgin Goddess. (The other Greek deities more usually thought of as Virgin Goddesses are Artemis, Athena, and Hestia because none of them married or bore children though Athena did raise Erichthonius, the son of Hephaestus and the Earth or Gaia, as her own.)

In *The Way of the Rose*, an exploration of the Divine Feminine and the practice of the rosary, the authors Clark Strand and Perdita Finn stressed the life-restoring power of the Great Goddess and other feminine deities who have been designated as virginal: "The Great Goddess is a virgin in the same way that a forest is a virgin—able to call forth life from within herself with the help of nothing but the golden light of the Sun. . . .[The ancient goddesses] were not pure or chaste, but green and powerful . . . able to resurrect the land and remake the world with the coming of every spring."[10]

Although Aphrodite evolved from the Great Mother Goddess, and so carries that primary Goddess's regenerative powers, and although she bore children with both gods and mortals, she is rarely identified with the role of mother. As noted earlier, all goddesses, like all gods, are archetypes, and the archetypes pertaining to women who are mothers and those who are sexually active are almost always separate in the Greek pantheon. Unfortunately, this non-integrated view of women's sexuality and fertility has not yet been reconciled in our collective Western psyche.

Furthermore, while Aphrodite represents the valuing of pleasure for pleasure's sake, especially sexual pleasure, she is also associated with the valuing of sexuality as an initiatory experience into the realm of the sacred. This is an aspect of sexuality not usually attributed to her son Eros, the God of Love, who is primarily linked with sexual desire and its physical expression.

For Aphrodite, sex can be a means to address a greater variety of needs and feelings, including spiritual ones; her emphasis is never just on genitally focused sex and certainly not only on male-oriented genitally focused sex. Because of this, she is the goddess who has been most revered by women who engage in sexual practices, such as those from Tantric or Taoist traditions that recognize the divine potential of sexuality, as well as by courtesans and sex workers who see themselves as sacred practitioners of the erotic arts.

Finally, while Aphrodite is typically portrayed in stories and art as youthful, she is always fully a woman, never girlish, in her presentation. Such imaging aligns with the classical ideal of adult female beauty, which favored an appearance of youth over age, an ideal that has changed little over the centuries. But it also symbolizes Aphrodite's eternal fruitfulness and creative power, attributes that can be meaningful to mature as well as young women. At the same time, because contemporary Western culture so consistently fights against aging and dismisses the value of maturity, especially in women, we would benefit from seeing more positive images in the arts and media of women at all stages of life who are in touch with Aphrodite's energy and secure in their own senses of beauty and sensuality.

Aphrodite is usually portrayed as unapologetically sensuous in her attitude. This is beautifully reflected in Aphrodite of Knidos by Praxiteles (360–330 BCE), one of the first life-sized nude sculptures of a woman that appeared in Greek art. (Previously, only heroic male figures were the subject of nude sculptures.) The sculpture represents the Goddess preparing for, or perhaps emerging from, her purifying bath. It was created for the Temple of Aphrodite at Knidos (an ancient Greek city in what is now modern-day Turkey) and was apparently intended to elicit sexual reactions from male visitors to the temple. Unfortunately, the original artwork was destroyed in a fire in 475 CE. Many Roman copies remain, though they are said to lack the beauty of the original.

THE WORSHIP OF APHRODITE

For the ancient Greeks, Aphrodite personified love and beauty as a living deity. She was regularly honored through personal and group rituals enacted in homes, at public shrines and temples, and at large communal events. There were temples devoted to the Goddess throughout Greece and the Eastern Mediterranean, but her main cult centers were the islands of Cyprus and Cythera (Kythira in modern Greece) and the city of Corinth, where she was considered the protector deity.

Her best-known public celebration was the annual festival of Aphrodisia, reported variously as having been held in either the spring or midsummer. A commonly cited date is the fourth day of the month following the Summer Solstice: July 4 in the current Gregorian calendar. The festival took place in many towns and cities but was especially popular in Corinth, on Cyprus, and in the Attica region (which includes Athens). Several rituals have been associated with Aphrodisia. For example, the killing of a white dove to purify a temple altar (the only bloody sacrifice allowed during the festival), the offering to the celebrants of phallus-shaped bread and salt to represent the sea, and the worship of Aphrodite's image.

It was common practice for the Greeks to carry statues of gods and goddesses in their religious processions, and they would think of those representations not as inanimate stone figures but as living symbols that were energized by the spirit of the deity who was portrayed. It has also been said that during Aphrodisia, a woman acting as a surrogate, likely a prostitute, would submerge herself naked in a town's harbor in order to call forth the Goddess to revitalize the earth. Feasting, music, dancing, and revelry were important elements of Aphrodisia, as well as other temple rituals. Such practices were in stark contrast to those connected to the festival of Adonia. That festival generally had a more somber tone due to its focus on a reenactment of Aphrodite's mourning for the death of Adonis.

It is not surprising that Aphrodite had a great many devotees in ancient Greece given what we know about the circumscribed lives of women at the time. Specific information about the status of women in that culture is sparse, and what does exist was usually written by men. It is known that women from different social groups and geographical regions experienced different degrees of freedom, but in cities such as Athens, women's lives were highly constrained. We can assume that Aphrodite would have symbolized a form of sexual privilege, independence, and sovereignty that few Greek women of that era would ever personally experience.

The festivals and ceremonies dedicated to the Goddess or other deities would undoubtedly have been welcomed because they offered women opportunities for acceptable excursions into public. In general, virtuous women were meant to stay home, obey their husbands, and remain quiet, discreet, and generally invisible. The Athenian statesman Pericles (c. 500 BCE) is quoted as saying, "The greatest glory of a woman is to be least talked about by man, whether they are praising you or criticizing you."[11] Men, meanwhile, were free to engage in the public sphere or travel according to their inclinations and station in life and frequently availed themselves either of prostitutes or *pornai*—of which there were many of both sexes—and courtesans or *hetaerae*. (The Greek names *pornai*, as well as *hetaerae*, *hetaira*, and similar variations, are still used by many historians to refer to two classes of prostitutes in ancient Greece. The former worked in brothels or on the street and typically had many clients, whereas the latter might have only a single or very few clients at any one time. The *hetaerae* were usually well-educated and cultured and often provided companionship and intellectual stimulation as well as sex.)[12]

Marriage for both partners was typically a loveless but socially unavoidable institution. The statesman Demosthenes (384–322 BCE) summed up the subject of women and marriage from men's perspective: "Mistresses we keep for pleasure, concubines for daily attendance upon our persons, and wives to bear us legitimate children and be our housekeepers."[13] Unlike men, women were expected to be faithful to their spouses. A woman who dishonored her husband and family through infidelity, thereby throwing into doubt the legitimacy of the male line, was guilty of the serious crime of *moicheia*, which would lead to her banishment from practicing in public religious ceremonies.[14] According to Karen Armstrong, the male establishment of Athens found women's impassioned participation in the festival of Adonia particularly distasteful because they viewed Adonis as personifying a man who never separated from the world of women and who represented the opposite of their elevated sober male ethos.[15]

Women were the most frequent visitors to Aphrodite's temples, particularly young women who wished to secure the Goddess's blessings for a favorable marriage. They would bring offerings such as statues, gold, jewelry, and animals for sacrifice. Many historians assert that men also visited the temples, often to engage sexually with the resident priestesses who were trained in Aphrodite's mysteries, including the art of physical love. The priestesses in these temples, sometimes called sacred prostitutes, were considered to be physical embodiments of Aphrodite endowed with the Goddess's virginal powers. The sexual engagement between a priestess and her partner was an enactment of the mystical union of feminine and masculine energies. Each would thereby transcend their personal selves to experience the divine.

This sacred rite was likely not confined to the temples of ancient Greece. Author Jalaja Bonheim pointed out that in ancient India, sexual priestesses who were raised, educated, and supported in temples were similarly considered embodiments of the goddess and called *devadasis*, meaning "servants of the Divine" or "servants of the Light." Any man who ritually made love to a *devadasi* became a god—the goddess's divine counterpart—through their sacred union.[16]

The temple of Corinth, considered to have been the principal temple to Aphrodite, is said to have had such priestesses (some sources say over a thousand) though that was not the case in all her temples. Temple priestesses—and perhaps the *hetaerae* who lived in the larger society—were also thought to carry knowledge of the healing arts and could prescribe herbs and practices that were important to women's health. Women might be drawn to life in the temples for a variety of reasons, including wanting to avoid either marriage or an unmarried life of chastity or because they felt called to serve a goddess. These priestesses were educated and given social status and, in some cases, were considered politically and legally equal to men.[17]

While temple priestesses or sacred prostitutes generally enjoyed more privileges than most women outside of the
temples, by all reports the *pornai*—the profane or secular prostitutes—had extremely restricted and difficult lives. Author
Nancy Qualls-Corbett told us that "Prostitution outside the
precincts of the temple was . . . apparently a cruel and brutal-
izing sport. The degradation of the profane prostitute—who
represents the dark side of feminine sexuality—was profound;
she was the very antithesis of the sacred prostitute, whose sexuality revered the goddess; yet they existed in juxtaposition."[18]

Some historians have rejected the use of the term "sacred
prostitution" as applied to practices of sacred sexuality in
Greece or elsewhere because it perpetuates the image of a temple priestess as one whose livelihood depended on catering to
men's desires. Others have disputed the very existence of sacred
prostitutes or sexual priestesses anywhere in the ancient world
and have contended that the case for their presence is based
on flawed research.[19] That may be true, at least in part, but it is
also worth considering whether the arguments against accept-
ing that women took on such roles devalue the transformative
power of the Divine Feminine in the sexual realm.

What other more general rites occurred in the temples to
Aphrodite and other deities is also not conclusive due to the
unreliability of many historical sources. It is broadly accepted,
however, that animals and other offerings were commonly taken
there to be burnt in sacrificial fires; the smoke from the fires was
believed to carry the prayers of the devoted to the goddesses
and gods on Olympus. Much of what is viewed as factual about

temple practices is drawn from the works of the writer Pausinias (110–180 CE) who left accounts of his travels throughout the Eastern Mediterranean. Some of the details he recorded specifically about Aphrodite's temples were that pigs were a common sacrifice (other than during the days of Aphrodisia), that the sacrificial fires were tended by priestesses and built with aromatic juniper wood to which special tree leaves would be added, and that only limited numbers of the public, if any, were allowed into the temples' innermost sanctums.[20]

Similar to the seduction of Eros is that of Aphrodite: the seduction of beauty. More beautiful than any other goddess ... Aphrodite is consecrated to love. This is her main occupation, the task assigned to her by the Moiras, the goddesses of destiny (Graves, 1955, 61). In this context, the goddess represented a cosmological force, without which life would be impossible. Aphrodite is the personification of vital energy. Thus myths inevitably describe her as intent on loving and seducing, also the merit of her magic girdle which no one can resist. In the Hellenistic view, her seduction is never dark and chthonic, as is the seduction of Pan. Only the tie with the pre-Hellenic Great Goddess—of whom, like Demeter and Artemis, she appears the manifestation— renders her the Mistress of Life and Death.

—ALDO CAROTENUTO, *Rites and Myths of Seduction*

Aphrodite's arrival in the world originated from a chaotic and violent act: Cronos taking revenge on his father's uncontrolled lust by cutting off his genitals and casting them into the sea. But as a result of that terrible event, something wonderful occurred. Uranus's genitals magically turned into foam in the water, and from that foam, the Goddess of Love and Beauty was born.

From the moment ancient poets described Aphrodite stepping gracefully onto the shores of Cyprus, she has held an honored place in our imaginations. To this day, she remains a complex, enigmatic, and beloved goddess throughout the Western world—one with the power to benevolently propagate life, love, and beauty, and to transform our lives for the better. However, Aphrodite's powers of transformation will only become manifest if we cultivate the appropriate attitude toward her. If we do not, we may suffer the consequences of an encounter with her shadow side.

Chapter 3

She Is the Golden One/She Is the Dark One

If the Cyprian falls on us, it's no good
Resisting. If we yield, she will come on us
Gently. If she finds us disdainful, she will
Abuse us O you can't think how severely.
She ranges the sky, she is there in the waves
Of the sea. Of the Cyprian all things were
Born. It is she who sows and gives love by
Which all of us on the earth have our being.

—EURIPIDES, *Hippolytus*

As the Goddess of Love and Beauty, Aphrodite is often referred to as the Golden One, an honorific meant to denote her special status as a divinity whose attributes of feminine wisdom, beauty, love, and regenerative power are manifested in bodily form. Aphrodite is envisioned as being as radiant as gold and like that precious metal, free from contamination.

Gold has long been considered an exalted element associated with the highest level of spiritual consciousness. In the ancient art of alchemy, the creation of gold was the culmination of the transformative process and symbolized the attainment of perfection and the integration of body, mind, and spirit. Aphrodite's "goldenness" or perfected consciousness is not only spiritual in nature. Because she is so deeply connected to feeling and relatedness, her consciousness can also be understood as having an earthly component, albeit one that has been exalted to the highest level of purity.[1]

But Aphrodite also has a shadow side that earned her the less flattering titles of the Dark One, the Deceptive One, the Unholy One, the Goddess of Destruction, and the Killer of Men among others. Although harsh, these titles reflect truths about Aphrodite's nature. They also mirror—in exaggerated form—truths about the shadow aspect of human nature.

Many myths record that Aphrodite could be jealous, deceptive, and manipulative if her desires were threatened or thwarted, and she would deal severely with those who failed to adequately honor her. One of many stories of Aphrodite's retribution involves Hippolytus, a young prince of Troizenos, who eschewed love and sexual pleasure and scorned her worship, dedicating himself instead to the goddess Artemis. Aphrodite responded by causing Hippolytus's stepmother Phaedra to fall in love with him. That resulted in Hippolytus's cruel rejection of Phaedra, Phaedra's suicide, and his father Theseus's placement of a curse on his son, which eventually led to Hippolytus's death.

Aphrodite also punished the women of Lemnos for their refusal to worship her by afflicting them with such a terrible odor that their husbands abandoned them. In a further act of revenge, Aphrodite caused the women to murder their husbands. Another of the Goddess's punitive measures was her treatment of Nerites, a young nymph who was her lover during the time she spent in the sea. When he declined to accompany Aphrodite to Mount Olympus, preferring to stay with his family, she turned him into a shellfish.

Probably the most famous myth involving Aphrodite's jealousy is that of the trials of Psyche. It is a long myth and rich in symbolism and wisdom regarding women's psychological development. A quick summary describes Psyche as a young woman so beautiful and so identified with Aphrodite that people worshipped her rather than the Goddess. Affronted, Aphrodite told her son Eros to make Psyche fall in love with someone vile, but Eros fell in love with Psyche himself and kept their affair secret from his mother. Eros tried to hide his identity from Psyche, but she found out and he fled. Psyche then appealed to Aphrodite for help. The Goddess, furious at both Psyche and Eros, gave Psyche a series of seemingly impossible tasks, but after many hardships, Psyche was able to complete them and reunite with Eros. Among other meanings, the myth is a cautionary tale of the inadvisability of identifying too strongly with an archetype.

Aphrodite's vengeful acts against those who she felt offended or dishonored her could be judged as extreme, but she was certainly not alone among the goddesses and gods in expressing wrath in violent ways. Also, the negative epithets thrown at her from usually male critics may have less to do with their assessment of Aphrodite's acts of vengeance than with their anger at her sense of autonomy (she will not be dominated by any man) and their jealousy and fear of her sexual power (to which they might easily fall victim), as well as her willingness to wield that power unabashedly. In the words of author Arianna Huffington, Aphrodite's energy is able to overcome reason and sink men "into the deepest morass of sensuality and [lift] them to the exaltation of cosmic union."[2] Her power is so great in the sexual realm that it has frightened men throughout the ages who have then rejected her—and any woman who embodies that power—because of it:

> . . . Marcello Ficino's harangue against the goddess in Renaissance Florence is the classic attack of a man's reason against a power that overwhelms it: "Only Venus comes on openly as your friend, and is secretly your enemy. You should be attacking her if you are going to be attacking any of the gods . . . She promises you her deadly pleasures and promises more than she ever delivers." . . . Aphrodite the enchantress . . . [is] the force men most fear and to which, at the same time, they are most irresistibly drawn. Those who try hardest to resist, those who imagine themselves immune to her power, are the ones on whom the goddess' wrath descends most vigorously: "Do not imagine you can abdicate," W. H. Auden's Venus warns. "Before you reach the frontier you are caught."[3]

The playwright Euripides struck a similar note many centuries before in *Hippolytus* (428 BCE), his tragedy about the doomed son of Theseus referenced earlier. In that play, Euripides holds Hippolytus accountable for his arrogance—though not for his cruelty toward his stepmother—but concludes that the principal destructive force at work in the lives of Hippolytus and those around him is unrestrained sexual desire. Thus, the responsibility for the play's tragic series of events is placed squarely at the feet of Aphrodite.

Every man carries within him the eternal image of woman, not the image of this or that particular woman, but a definite feminine image. This image is fundamentally unconscious, an hereditary factor of primordial origin engraved in the living organic system of the man, an imprint or "archetype" of all the ancestral experiences of the female [called the anima]... The same is true of the woman: she too has her inborn image of man [called the animus]... Hence most of what men say about feminine eroticism, and particularly about the emotional life of women, is derived from their own anima projections and distorted accordingly. On the other hand, the astonishing assumptions and fantasies that women make about men come from the activity of the animus...

—CARL JUNG, *The Development of the Personality*

FATAL ATTRACTION

As male deities gradually took precedence in the religions of the Western world, women's societal value came to be seen as subordinate to that of men. Not only did this shift result in the removal of goddesses as an appropriate focus of worship and the displacement of women from the practice of religious rites, but sexuality in general came to be viewed as evil and sinful except for the purposes of procreation. In particular, women's sexuality, which was once considered a divinely inspired and transformative aspect of women's nature, was increasingly dismissed, denounced, and degraded by the new religious authorities and the populace who followed their edicts. In the words of Jungian psychologist James Hillman, Western consciousness "has never known what to do with the dark, material, and passionate part of itself, except to cast it off and call it Eve."[4]

An enduring symbol of society's anxieties regarding women's sexual power is the figure of the femme fatale, who is seen as alluring but dangerous. Eve as the evil temptress is only one representation of the femme fatale or the dark side of Aphrodite. Other examples from history and literature are Salome, Delilah, Mata Hari, and John Keats's "La Belle Dame sans Merci," to name only a few. Many women reject this role, but some are attracted to it; it is one of the few roles in a male-dominated society in which women can experience being sexual, powerful, and in control at the same time.

But in truth, the femme fatale archetype has always been more about men's insecurities than women's sexual freedom. Whether projected onto a real woman or a fictional character, the femme fatale is both desired and feared by men and some women as well. She is captivating because she is untamable, but they know she will inevitably lead to their destruction. Men therefore need to protect themselves against her even as they lust after her. The author Mickey Spillane (said to have created the modern prototype in his crime novels) pithily summed her up as "the kind of girl you can punch right in the mouth with your lips."[5]

Femme fatales are especially easy to identify in the film noir genre from the 1940s and 1950s, a genre that reflected the era's social anxieties about sexuality and the role of women. This almost requisite character was often contrasted with a virtuous "damsel in distress" (a correspondingly limiting role for a woman) and paired with a weak or shamed man reminiscent of Hephaestus. Symbolic representations of Aphrodite's shadow continue to be included in movies, novels, and other artifacts of popular culture, although usually not quite as blatantly as in film noir. The following description of the femme fatale is from ApolloPad, an internet site providing information and resources for new writers: "This stock character . . . is to be ultimately feared and condemned. . . . Typically, her power is not a brute strength but lies in traditionally 'feminine' powers such as her charm and heightened sexuality, which the archetypal femme fatale uses to get what she wants."[6]

"The American Plan" is a real-life case in point of the injurious consequences that can befall individuals and society at large when the femme fatale archetype is projected en masse. Under that now nearly forgotten "social hygiene" campaign of the last century, thousands of women (up to hundreds of thousands according to some estimates) were imprisoned by the United States government, usually without due process, from the 1910s to the 1950s. The women affected were not only unfairly incarcerated but were also frequently subjected to unwanted and invasive health procedures simply because they were suspected by officials of being prostitutes, carrying STDs, or just being "promiscuous."[7]

Another pertinent historical example of how society has failed to handle its deep discomfort with female sexuality was the media and public reaction to the publication in 1976 of *The Hite Report: A National Study of Female Sexuality* by American social historian Shere Hite.[8] *The Hite Report* was based on a detailed survey of over one hundred thousand women about their experiences of sex. Among Hite's conclusions—considered highly controversial at the time—were that sex is culturally rather than biologically driven and that society's attitudes needed to change to accommodate women's sexual desires and preferences.

Hite's findings were greeted eagerly by many women (though less so by many men). They also prompted immediate and virulent criticism from a variety of quarters. The book and the author herself were frequently met with vitriol, dismissive laughter, and charges of being anti-male by reviewers, commentators, and members of the public (particularly conservative religious groups).

After *The Hite Report*, Hite went on to author several other books about sexuality and gender relations, but unfortunately, she was unable to transcend the ongoing scrutiny and misogynistic abuse she suffered from her critics (she even received death threats). She eventually fled to Europe and from public view, and her work was largely forgotten for several decades. Hite died in 2020, but her contributions to an understanding of human sexuality, particularly women's sexuality, have now returned to the spotlight through a film about her life, *The Disappearance of Shere Hite* (2023) by Nicole Newnham. In the words of film critic Monica Castillo, "In essence, [Hite] was slut shamed out of history, and we are forced to reckon with that loss . . . [But] Newnham's documentary mourns and celebrates this impressive figure so that future generations will understand why she—and the work she pioneered—still matter."[9]

OVERIDENTIFICATION WITH THE GODDESS

The examples just cited speak specifically to Aphrodite's sexual and erotic power over men and their conflicted and usually unconscious responses to it. But Aphrodite's power can also affect women if they are involved sexually with another woman who is carrying intense Aphrodite energy, especially if they have not developed and integrated the Aphrodite aspect of their own personality. Like men, women can feel transported by the sense of fulfillment promised by such an archetypal encounter. And like men, they may fear being overwhelmed by their feelings and may be highly vulnerable to the demands of the woman who is evoking those feelings.

Women who themselves identify strongly with the Goddess

can also be negatively affected by the magnitude of her psychological power. There is a great difference between identifying *with* an archetype and identifying *as* an archetype. The first can catalyze the growth of undeveloped aspects of the self; the second can lead to self-aggrandizement and manipulation of others to bolster one's self-esteem and serve one's ego needs. It can also contribute to the under-development of other aspects of the self as represented by Aphrodite's sister goddesses.

The experience of archetypal energy in our lives can be numinous, awe-inspiring, and life-changing. A direct experience of Aphrodite, which might occur when we are in love or transported by beauty, can leave us feeling radiant, joyful, and fully alive. But archetypal *overidentification* (when a person sees themselves as a literal embodiment of the archetype), whether conscious or unconscious, inevitably brings suffering.

Women who overidentify with Aphrodite commonly feel great loss, even desperation, when they think they no longer live up to an Aphrodisian ideal of physical beauty, especially as they age. Multiple beauty treatments, facelifts, and extreme diet and exercise regimens are not uncommon consequences of an over-identification with the Goddess. This experience can befall the type of woman Jungian theorists describe as an "anima woman," one who at some level agrees to become a personification of a man's *anima*—his unconscious eternal image of woman and his feminine soul—and may become overly attached to her power to attract, influence, and manipulate him. Hollywood has given us many examples of women who have accepted the archetypal projection of Aphrodite to their own detriment. The tragic life of

Marilyn Monroe, often referred to as a love goddess, is a famous case. Sadly, women who have adopted this role can never feel secure that they are accepted and loved for their true selves and not for their contrived presentations.

Not surprisingly, an anima woman is rarely well-received by other women, particularly those whose partners are fascinated with her. In contrast, a woman who has a good relationship with the principle of eros, in the sense of relatedness and a mature and integrated "inner-Aphrodite," likely has a strong sense of self, is not dependent on the outside world to mirror back her value, and has better connections with others. That said, even women who themselves have a healthy relationship with Aphrodite may still elicit jealousy, fear, and anger from women and men who have not integrated their own multi-faceted feminine natures.

For an Aphrodite woman, Eros's arrow can pierce at any time. If one is made of the stuff of the goddess of love, one may have no choice but to obey Aphrodite. Such a woman has much less choice in how she behaves that she—or others—imagine. The more archetypally identified our nature, the less our sense of choice. We are then pulled by fate.

—ARLENE DIANE LANDAU, *Tragic Beauty*

Another problematic aspect of an overidentification with Aphrodite can be an acceptance of emotional powerlessness in love. In some of her myths, Aphrodite is presented as holding her own in relationships; that is, she surrenders to her feelings of attraction or love but never forgets who she is or what power she possesses. Indeed, she often wields that power in order to control aspects of those relationships.

In some of her affairs, however, especially those with Ares and Adonis, Aphrodite appears to forego all other concerns to focus her attention on her passion for her lovers. In each case, this choice leaves her emotionally vulnerable, and in the case of Adonis, she suffers immensely when he dies. On the one hand, Aphrodite's behavior in these intense relationships speaks to the necessity of relinquishing ego control in order to fully experience love for another. On the other, it cautions women in particular not to become so absorbed in or identified with another person that they abandon a sense of themselves in service to a romantic fantasy.

Finally, in contrast to an overidentification with Aphrodite, Homer identified three related figures over whom Aphrodite had no power—positive or negative. These were Athena, Goddess of Wisdom and Crafts; Artemis, Goddess of the Hunt; and Hestia, Goddess of the Hearth. While all other deities and mortals were subject to Aphrodite's charms even though their relationships with her were often conflictual, these three goddesses were seen as being beyond her powers because they had little use for them. This same attitude can be observed in women who are generally indifferent to what Aphrodite represents because their interests and attentions lie elsewhere. But as with women who are overidentified with Aphrodite, too much emphasis on the concerns of only one goddess and the dismissal of what other goddesses have to offer can limit self-development.

At the end of Chapter 2, I mentioned the importance of cultivating an appropriate attitude toward Aphrodite. Given the force and intensity of Aphrodite's shadow side, it follows that the optimal attitude to take toward her is one of deep and loving respect, coupled perhaps with a hearty dose of discernment when it comes to making personal behavioral and relationship choices.

The preceding diverse examples—those derived from Aphrodite's myths and those from historical and contemporary contexts—all point to the necessity of understanding the potentially negative as well as the positive effects of this Goddess's great power. Anyone who ignores, denigrates, or underestimates Aphrodite will pay dearly for it, as is clearly portrayed in her myths. When figures such as Hippolytus, Psyche, or the women of Lemnos dishonored her, Aphrodite punished them without hesitation. In real-life circumstances, Aphrodite's acts of "vengeance" may not be as immediately obvious, but they are no less consequential.

For instance, through the ages, innumerable cultural, religious, and government leaders, as well as domestic tyrants, have demonstrated their deep-seated fear of women's sexuality and autonomy—especially their sexual autonomy—by way of enforcing restrictive gender roles and policing and condemning any of women's sexual behaviors that they deemed to be "improper" or "dangerous." Aphrodite's responses to such offenses against her spirit have usually been of a psychological and emotional nature. Instead of magical punishments on a mythological scale, we may typically observe unhappiness, tension, conflict, and distorted emotional and sexual relationships in the lives of individual perpetrators, as well as in society at large. In the end, no one escapes unaffected after offending a goddess as powerful as Aphrodite. Unfortunately, the targets of Aphrodite's transgressors inevitably suffer also, even more so if they internalize their victimizers' oppressive beliefs.

As discussed earlier, our failure to align with Aphrodite's values of love and beauty can seriously impede our psychological and spiritual development. But that failure can be subtle, and this is where discernment about where we direct our attention and energy is necessary. Here is a simple example: To place continued and undue emphasis—even through humor—on the notion that there is a never-ending and insurmountable "war between the sexes" can fortify problematic stereotypes of women and men and the nature of the relationships that are possible between them.

Ideally, we need to mitigate feelings of division and animosity between the sexes (as between all peoples), not foster them. Our challenge now, in order to heal and grow, is to discover new and more integrated ways of relating to one another and the world. This can be accomplished in part through opening ourselves to the propitious transformative power of the "Golden One."

Women who identify with the archetype of Aphrodite on a personality level (that is, they feel that Aphrodite is already a dominant archetype in their lives) or want to develop more of their Aphrodite nature in a healthy way, may wish to explore this subject in more depth. Men, whether or not they are in a relationship with a woman who identifies with Aphrodite, may also like to increase their understanding of that archetype.

Four popular books I recommend for this purpose are *Goddesses in Everywoman: A New Psychology of Women* (2014) and *Gods in Everyman: A New Psychology of Men's Lives and Loves* (2014) both by Jean Shinoda Bolen; *Gods and Goddesses in Love: Making the Myth a Reality for You* (2004) by Agapi Stassinopoulos; and *The Goddess Within: A Guide to the Eternal Myths that Shape Women's Lives* (1989) by Jennifer Barker Woolger and Roger Woolger.[10]

Although all of these books were published some time ago, the information in them is still relevant. A more recent publication that speaks to the problems that can be associated with the archetype of Aphrodite is *Tragic Beauty: The Dark Side of Venus Aphrodite and the Loss and Regeneration of Soul* (2019) by Arlene Diane Landau.[11] There are also many online sites that address both the positive and negative aspects of this archetype.

Chapter 4

Aphrodite's Transformative Powers

If you want to know the secrets of the universe,

think in terms of energy, frequency, and vibration.

—NIKOLA TESLA, as quoted by Ralph Bergstresser

Another of Aphrodite's many titles is the Alchemical Goddess. To fully appreciate the significance and value of her power in our lives, we need to understand the true meaning of that designation.

Alchemy is the ancient art of transformation and is most commonly understood as the practice of transmuting base metal into gold. From the standpoint of modern physical science, alchemy is acknowledged as the forerunner of chemistry but is typically dismissed as a misguided and arcane pursuit. From the perspective of psychology and spirituality, however, alchemy can be seen as a metaphor and a map for the process one undergoes in creating one's inner "gold" (that is, one's true self), and its stages mirror those of the process of "individuation," Carl Jung's term for becoming one's fully integrated self. The alchemical vision is one of unity, inclusiveness, and a balanced relationship between opposites—including between feminine and masculine energies—both in regard to individuals and the world. For Aphrodite to be named the Alchemical Goddess is to recognize her exceptional power to effect transformation in our lives through love and beauty, her two domains of greatest influence.

We experience the alchemy of Aphrodite when we feel drawn toward another person and fall in love; we feel it when we are touched by her power of transformation and creativity; we know it when we appreciate the capacity we have to make what we focus on beautiful and valued because it is infused with our love. Whatever is ordinary and undeveloped is the "baser" material of everyday life, which can be turned into "gold" through Aphrodite's creative alchemical influence . . .

—JEAN SHINODA BOLEN, *Goddesses in Everywoman*

A MODEL OF THE TRANSFORMATIVE PROCESS

Countless volumes have been written about the healing and transformative powers of love in its many forms. Such is the message of all great spiritual traditions, and I do not review those here, though in the next chapter, I do expand on the power of *embodied* love as related to Aphrodite's teachings. In subsequent chapters, I also address specific aspects of the transformative power of beauty. But first, I will briefly shift course and look at the mechanism of change that is at work through Aphrodite's ministrations.

It is easy to accept that experiences of both love and beauty can be transformative, but it might not be clear just *how* they serve to transform us. From a strictly psychological point of view, those experiences are impactful because they are able to change our mental or emotional state—for instance, to move us from sadness to surprise or joy. A metaphysical perspective is that those same experiences can alter our consciousness by raising our vibrational frequency. If we focus our attention on the higher-order frequencies of love and beauty, we will raise our own frequency to those levels and, in turn, attract the same frequencies. This is what it means to create your own reality.

One researcher and writer whose work sheds light on how our focus of attention (including our thoughts and emotions) determines our experience is David R. Hawkins. In *Power vs. Force: The Hidden Determinants of Human Behavior*, Hawkins, a former psychiatrist, presented a detailed map, which categorizes and ranks the fields of energy associated with different levels of consciousness.[1] His map starts with the experience of shame at the lowest level and moves upward to the experience of enlightenment at the highest level. (Reproductions of this map can easily be found online.) Whether or not Hawkins's approach has yielded the definitive map of consciousness, his rankings make intuitive sense—the states of consciousness listed at the bottom just *feel* heavier than the ones at the top—and so the map he created can be a useful guide to understanding how one can grow emotionally and spiritually through cultivating higher-order experiences like love and the appreciation and creation of beauty.

Keep in mind that Hawkins's scale is logarithmic rather than linear so even a small progression in one's level can have a large effect. (A logarithmic scale displays in a compact way numerical data that increases in value at an exponential rather than a linear rate.) Furthermore, as Hawkins and other researchers have emphasized, the power of consciousness is such that each individual who advances their personal level counterbalances a much greater degree of negativity or lesser consciousness in the population at large.

As outlined in Chapter 1, a major shift in consciousness is taking place worldwide and as a result, increasing numbers of people are reviewing their lives and values, and making changes to live more authentically and joyfully, and with a greater sense of meaning and purpose. Each such positive change, however small, contributes to raising the general consciousness of all of us, which bodes well for our collective future. At the same time, it can be expected that many people will experience intense lower vibrational emotions like grief and anger as they confront the reality that they have been lied to and manipulated throughout their lives by individuals and systems that they have trusted (including religious and spiritual systems). Having to face betrayals of such magnitude can lead to deep depression and moving out of such a state can be very difficult.

However, the more someone is willing to take responsibility for their emotional experience, the more chance there is for them to heal. Although the distressing external events that produced their depression may have been out of their control, each individual retains the ability to choose their response to what has affected them. Strong support for this idea was provided by psychiatrist Victor Frankl who, in *Man's Search for Meaning*, described his imprisonment in a German concentration camp in World War II.[2] Frankl's experiences led him to conclude that even in the most desperate of conditions an individual has "a choice of action" and that they "*can* preserve a vestige of spiritual freedom, of independence of mind, even in . . . terrible conditions of psychic and physical stress." In his view, "everything can be taken from a man but one thing: the last of the human freedoms—to choose one's attitude in any given set of circumstances, to choose one's own way."[3]

There are two essential keys to "choosing one's own way" in order to keep moving forward and "upward" in terms of vibration and consciousness: First, it is important to stay connected to one's values, and second, to adopt attitudes and behaviors that promote emotional and spiritual growth and resilience. In short, raising one's consciousness is the ultimate "inside job" accomplished by choosing carefully *what* one attends to, *how* one attends to it, and *how* one expresses oneself in the world as a result. That said, attainment of higher levels of consciousness is usually a slow process no matter what methods one follows or what scale of measurement one uses, though more rapid advancement may be achieved through involvement in practices specifically designed to heighten one's spiritual awareness and reverence for life.

It is now time to return to where this chapter began—the recognition of Aphrodite's alchemical powers—and highlight a transformational practice that anyone can adopt, even in the most challenging of circumstances: that is, to commit to identifying experiences of love and beauty in all their varied manifestations. This practice could be as simple as noticing and appreciating experiences of love and beauty when and where they occur. Or it could be made more active by engaging in pursuits intended to generate such experiences for the benefit of oneself or others. The ongoing practice of seeking and expressing love and beauty, in whatever form, can lead to a profound, long-lasting, and life-enhancing upward shift in one's vibrational frequency and overall level of consciousness.

Aphrodite invites us to stay connected at all times to our hearts and our senses. If we choose to respond to that invitation, we will receive the blessings of her abundant alchemical powers: healing, growth, transformation, and a joyful existence.

Love transforms one into what one loves.

—ST. CATHERINE OF SIENA, *The Dialogue*

A Personal Story

The experience of beauty as a path of healing and transformation has special resonance and meaning for me. Throughout my life, I have followed what I call a "beauty path" dedicated to the discovery and experience of beauty wherever I can find it. This has been a personal journey shaped over many years of individual exploration and research devoted to fostering my own and my clients' psychological and spiritual growth.

My chosen path is not related to any formal system and has no clearly definable stages or easily measured markers of success, though in retrospect, I am able to discern both. (A disclaimer: I privately used the name "beauty path" for my experience long before I discovered the traditional Navajo-Diné concept of a "beauty way path." I discuss the Navajo-Diné's more encompassing concept in subsequent chapters.) What follows is an example of when I chose to purposefully attend to the beauty around me and allowed a deep experience of that beauty to transform my negative emotions into ones of appreciation, gratitude, and a sense of peace.

In early 2020 when I initially heard that a dangerous virus was loose in the world and that immediate and drastic action needed to be taken by everyone everywhere to combat it, like most people, I was taken aback and fearful. But I also felt skeptical about the story being put forth by the media and the government (in my case, the Canadian government) about a deadly global pandemic. I clearly remember the moment in March of that year when a friend and I turned to each other and agreed there was something fishy about that narrative. It seemed too quickly established, too slick, and too coordinated. It took some months before I would begin to see the bigger picture and understand why events had unfolded as they had.

continued

I am generally an optimistic and resilient person, and I strive to maintain a high spiritual vibration, but as increased restrictions were put into place and I learned more about the nefarious driving forces behind them, I began to feel afraid for my own and our collective future. The official predictions of mass infection and casualties didn't ring true to me, and I was not worried that either I or my loved ones would become ill, but I did grow more and more concerned about the loss of our civil rights and liberties.

Thankfully, I found a number of alternative internet-based news sources that explored those concerns in depth, as well as much else about the pandemic and the more general world situation. That information was crucial in helping me connect the dots about what was going on, but it was also often frightening and depressing. I soon realized I needed to find something else to focus on to shift my energy when my thoughts started to spiral downward.

As I have done before when I have felt troubled, I turned to beauty—this time as an antidote to the dark and often shocking truths I was encountering in my internet deep dives. Discovering and celebrating beauty has not only been a constant source of pleasure in my life but has reliably provided comfort when I have needed it. So, on the first day of spring 2020 (an auspicious day for starting something new), I began a Beauty Diary. Every day I would seek out an experience of beauty. That experience might be one that overtly involved my senses—the brilliant pink and orange palette of a sunset over the ocean or the perfume of an abundant yellow rose bush I passed on a meandering neighborhood walk—or one that involved other people such as an uplifting talk with a simpatico friend or a video by someone who was sharing a controversial perspective—an example of beautiful courage.

My diary entries varied in length, but they all served the

purpose of directing my attention to what felt positive and healing in the midst of the chaos, confusion, and fear I was watching build around me. I ceased keeping the diary after a few months but only when I felt more spiritually centered, felt sure that salutary and concrete outer changes were underway (that the forces of light were slowly but surely overcoming the forces of darkness), and when I decided to turn my attention to writing this book, an experience that in itself allowed me to immerse myself in the subject of beauty. But I have not stopped scanning my environment for examples of beauty—nor do I expect I ever will—either for the simple pleasure of doing so or if I need to connect with a greater spiritual healing power.

Chapter 5

Eros, Sex, and Desire

The madness of love is the greatest of heaven's blessings.

—PLATO, *Phaedrus*

S ome Greek creation myths claim that Eros existed before Aphrodite. Others say that Aphrodite gave birth to Eros either with Ares as his father or parthenogenically. Whatever his origin, Eros and Aphrodite are inextricably linked by virtue of their shared rulership over the domain of love. But they are not simply male and female counterparts in that domain; each embodies different aspects of the experience of love. Also, Eros's rulership does not extend to beauty as Aphrodite's does.

In most myths, Eros's role is to induce love and sexual desire in those whom he targets with his arrows, primarily to promote procreation. His focus is not on the personal feelings that love evokes but on love's attendant physiological urges. Aphrodite's intent, on the other hand, is to promote courtship, pleasure, and tenderness, as well as sensual expressions of love that could—but do not necessarily—result in off-spring. Nevertheless, it is Eros that has become synonymous with our general experience of romantic and sexual love. (Unfortunately, our associations with Cupid, the Roman version of Eros, have not fared well over time. His image is now typically reduced to that of a plump, winged, diaper-clad boy who appears mischievously wielding his bow and arrow every February 14.)

Although Eros was originally associated with sexual desire and physical expressions of love, we have come to use the terms derived from his name, "eros" and "erotic," much more expansively. The way those words are now understood extends beyond bodily impulses to romantic and spiritual feelings. In this respect, our current idea of eros has come to incorporate aspects of love and its transformative spiritual power that were in earlier times more closely associated with Aphrodite.

In philosophy and psychology, eros has also come to denote the even more inclusive concept of "life energy" or "life instinct," in contrast to *thanatos*, the "death instinct" or "death drive," as theorized by Sigmund Freud. For example, Denis de Rougemont, in his classic work *Love in the Western World*, defined *eros* as a dynamic spiritual drive as opposed to Christian love or *agape* (the pure and selfless love that God has for us and that we are meant to have for others): "[Eros is] complete desire, luminous aspiration, the primitive religious soaring carried to its loftiest pitch . . . The erotic process introduces into life . . . a desire that never relapses, that nothing can satisfy . . . It is *infinite transcendence*."[1]

This is analogous to the ancient Greek concept of *pothos*, which refers to "the spiritual component of love or the erotic component of spirit" that Aphrodite inspired in her followers. To experience *pothos* is to experience deep longing for that which can never be possessed, but its intensity drives desire ever onward.[2]

A famous religious example that captures both de Rougemont's view of eros and the concept of *pothos* is the vision of the sixteenth-century Spanish mystic Teresa of Avila. She described her experience of spiritual ecstasy as follows:

> I saw in [an angel's] hand a long spear of gold, and at the iron's point there seemed to be a little fire. He appeared to me to be thrusting it at times into my heart, and to pierce my very entrails; when he drew it out, he seemed to draw them out also, and to leave me all on fire with a great love of God. The pain was so great, that it made me moan; and yet so surpassing was the sweetness of this excessive pain, that I could not wish to be rid of it. The soul is satisfied now with nothing less than God. The pain is not bodily, but spiritual; though the body has its share in it. It is a caressing of love so sweet which now takes place between the soul and God, that I pray God of His goodness to make him experience it who may think that I am lying.[3]

Gian Lorenzo Bernini's life-sized marble portrayal of Saint Teresa's moment of ecstasy, completed in 1652 and located in the Cornaro Chapel in the church of Santa Maria della Vittoria in Rome, is considered one of the sculptural masterpieces of the Baroque era.

If we take into consideration the just-mentioned expansive views of eros and understand the term to encompass romantic and spiritual feelings as well as the expression of physical desires, it follows that a true erotic—and also a true Aphrodisian—experience only exists in the context of a relationship that carries us in some way beyond our base instincts and egos through a genuine valuing of the "other," which leads toward an experience of connection and wholeness. A strictly needs-based sexual encounter, then, one without a true valuing of one's partner, could never be considered erotic because it would have no ego-transcendent potential. As the writer C. S. Lewis stated, "Sexual desire, without Eros, wants *it*, the *thing in itself*; Eros wants the Beloved . . . Without Eros, sexual desire, like every other desire, is a fact about ourselves."[4]

Nor does an erotic experience have to be limited to a sexual response as it is now commonly understood. An erotic experience, as dramatically illustrated by Teresa of Avila's angelic encounter, could be any physical, emotional, or spiritual event that evokes in us a valuing response to the beauty and mystery of life. Without such valuing, we are left with only transitory sensation and an inability to fully experience the power of Pleasure or Hedone, the child that resulted from the union of Eros and Psyche (who, after her marriage to Eros, became Goddess of the Soul). But with such valuing and the desire to increase it, we can create a deeply pleasurable and erotic life in which we are not only attuned to sensuality and beauty in the world but also to the possibility of ego-transcendence.

Sadly, the world in which we have been living has widely promoted the experience of superficial and unsatisfying sensation over true eroticism through an emphasis on consumerism and disposability in all aspects of life, including relationships and sexuality. This has resulted in a separation of body and spirit in the collective consciousness and a large-scale disconnection from soul. Needless to say, it has also contributed to the debasement of the principles and qualities accorded to Aphrodite and the Divine Feminine.

Proof of such debasement can be seen in the impaired relationship so many of us have with our bodies that inhibits our ability to know and express our own physical desires—as opposed to only being responsive to others' desires—and to fully embody and rejoice in our sexuality. This appears to be the case for a great many women, at least in the Western world, and it is the case for many men also. Author Caroline Knapp explored this subject in *Appetites: Why Women Want.* This is her reaction to seeing the cover of a *Shape* magazine that featured an impossibly perfect image of a popular movie actress:

> I look at this and sigh. Weight, weight, weight; abs, butt, thighs. Any woman with a modicum of self-awareness understands what this material is intended to do. It is goddess worship, goddess religion for the consumer age, commandments chiseled on skin and bone, and it is designed to whip us mere mortals into a frenzy of

inadequacy so potent it causes us to act, to go forth and buy the magazine and the many products it advertises. Thou shalt be thin, the goddess commands. Thou shalt not have wrinkles. Thou shalt compare and contrast. Thou shalt fail to measure up.[5]

The attitude promoted by such advertising—that of a narcissistic and manipulative pseudo-goddess—is, of course, antithetical to Aphrodite's essential nature. Yes, Aphrodite expressed anger and jealousy when others threatened her position as "the fairest," but that response was not born of insecurity; she never doubted her own beauty and value. What she considered to be violations by her adversaries were either their attempts to usurp her rightful position or their failures to adequately honor her. There would be no reason for Aphrodite (or one of her true devotees) to hide her passionate feelings and sexual desires or to be embarrassed about her appearance because there would never be shame attached to those experiences.

The erotic instinct is something questionable, and will always be so whatever a future set of laws may have to say on the matter. It belongs, on the one hand, to the original animal nature of man, which will exist as long as man has an animal body. On the other hand, it is connected with the highest forms of the spirit. But it blooms only when the spirit and instinct are in true harmony. If one or the other aspect is missing, then an

> injury occurs, or at least there is a one-sided lack of bal-
> ance which easily slips into the pathological. Too much
> of the animal disfigures the civilized human being, too
> much culture makes a sick animal.

—CARL JUNG, *Symbols of Transformation*

SACRED SEXUALITY

Aphrodite presides over all forms of love, but she is best known and most revered for the energy she brings to relationships that have a romantic or sexual component, regardless of whether those relationships conform to religious, social, or cultural norms. For Aphrodite, there is never sin attached to her choices. Her own liaisons, with the exception of her marriage to Hephaestus, which was decreed by Zeus, were based on love and desire rather than social approval or convention. These latter concerns fall more under the purview of Hera, Goddess of Marriage.

Also, while Aphrodite is associated with the general fruitfulness of the earth and fertility, her favored sexual liaisons do not necessarily have to result in the birth of children, though that could be a desired outcome. In this respect, Aphrodite's role as a fertility goddess is quite different from that of Demeter, Goddess of the Harvest, who is more associated with fertility as it pertains to mothering, as well as the land and its bounty, especially grain.

Aphrodite does not care whether or not she creates complications in the lives of those to whom she turns her attention. Her energy is that of nature fully and freely seeking to express itself. Aeschylus in his *Danaid* trilogy of plays (c. fifth century BCE), gave Aphrodite voice to express her purpose and power: "The holy heaven is full of desire to mate with the earth, and desire seizes the earth to find a mate; rain falls from the amorous heaven and impregnates the earth; and the earth brings forth for men the fodder of flocks and herds and the gifts of Demeter; and from the same moistening marriage-rite the fruit of trees is ripened. Of these things I am the cause."[6]

To surrender to the call of such heavenly-supported desire with an awakened sensibility can elevate love and sexual union to the realm of the sacred. This is achieved through the presence of what Carl Jung called a supraordinate "third" energy. A sexual union transformed by such an energy symbolizes the coming together of equal opposites—conceptualized variously as the Divine Feminine and Divine Masculine, Earth-Mother and Sky-Father, or Shakti and Shiva—in the archetypal *hieros gamos* or mystical marriage. This is a profound psychic process which, according to Jung, brings about "the 'earthing' of the spirit and the spiritualizing of the earth"[7] and is simultaneously manifested on three interconnected levels: interpersonally, intrapersonally, and transpersonally. Love, as an aspect of the divine, is what catalyzes and drives this process.

But to cultivate such an awakened sensibility regarding sexual expression runs counter to how sex has been secularized, commodified, and promoted in our modern world. This is reflected in the proliferation of pornography and the ubiquity of pornography-influenced messages in the mass media that minimize and devalue relatedness and foster increasingly casual attitudes toward sex. Ginette Paris, a social psychologist, wrote the following passage as part of a "meditation" on Aphrodite published in 1986. The situation she described then has not improved over the decades. In fact, it has worsened.

> . . . the sacred nature of sexuality has been expunged; and . . . laicized sex has become, in the minds of too many, the equivalent of a hygienic function or a social game. . . . Sex games certainly have their place among interesting leisure-time activities. But what has happened to sexuality as an initiation into the realm of the sacred? Must we borrow from the Tantric of the Orient to learn of illumination by the sexual path? No, we have in our own cultural past an alternative to both the Judeo-Christian attitude of sexual repression and its corollary, contemporary sexual promiscuity and the insignificance which accompanies it.[8]

Paris considered the prevalence of "laicized sex" (secularized sex) to be a lamentable by-product of the sexual revolution that began in the 1960s. That revolution, along with the feminist movement, can be rightfully credited for catalyzing much-needed scrutiny and rejection of some repressive societal forces, but in the ongoing quest for liberation and equality, the sacred aspect of sex and some important differences between women's and men's experiences of sex and intimacy have been minimized or ignored. No one, whatever one's sexual or gender identification, benefits from living in a society that emphasizes the commodification of sex or its secularization at the expense of its potential sanctity. The Divine Feminine is especially ill-served by such attitudes.

The Divine Feminine is similarly degraded by the opposite attitude: standards and practices that attempt to control sexuality, particularly women's sexuality. A contemporary example is the "purity movement" that arose during the early 1990s, primarily in the white American evangelical Christian community. That movement, as described by former member Linda Kay Klein, stipulates that both sexes adhere to strict stereotyped gender roles and that they maintain chastity by acts, thoughts, and feelings before marriage. Furthermore, a woman is taught that her body is evil (whereas men are taught that their minds are evil) and also that she is responsible for the sexual temptations of men.[9]

Of course, the purity movement is not the only religious movement that enforces such rules. Comparable gender- and sexually based restrictions can be found in many different countries and cultures. For example, Mormons use the word "worthiness" instead of "purity," and Muslims say "honor culture" rather than "purity culture." Although the terms used may vary, there is commonality in the underlying tenets of these and other religious traditions regarding the appropriate role and function of women's sexuality.

Clearly, the time has come for us to embrace alternative attitudes and behaviors in terms of love and sex that would serve as correctives to such control systems as well as the rampant over-sexualization and under-eroticism of our modern world. The alternative from "our own cultural past" (Western civilization's origin in ancient Greece) that Paris suggested we adopt is the true honoring of Aphrodite. Historical records contain numerous examples of when and how people have respected and celebrated the Goddess. We can turn to these in the present for inspiration (though not necessarily replication).

For instance, Sappho (c. 620–570 BCE), the famed poet from the island of Lesbos in Greece, was the leader of a *thisasos* or community of young women dedicated to religious education and the cultivation of refinement and grace. Being well-versed in such arts was considered essential to a good life, and she taught her students how to express themselves through speech, poetry, music, and dance. They were also tutored in the arts of seduction and love in preparation for marriage so that they could become Aphrodite's priestesses and guides to love's rituals within their relationships.

Whether or not any of the official priestesses in Aphrodite's temples practiced sacred prostitution, there is ample evidence that Aphrodite (as well as corresponding goddesses from other cultures) has been honored over time as the patron of secular prostitutes and courtesans, both by the women themselves and their admirers. Interestingly, images of Eros, Aphrodite, and Venus came into fashion during the European Renaissance, a time period when courtesans rose to cultural prominence. During that era, innumerable portrayals of the Goddess appeared, often created by the same artists who painted courtesans. In those images, Aphrodite and Venus were frequently surrounded by *éclats*—rosy bursts of light—and bore the like-ness of favored courtesans of the time.[10]

A more recent association between the Goddess and sex work was made by the escort Veronica Monet. She did not specifically name Aphrodite as her spiritual inspiration but clearly adopted Aphrodisian principles in her approach to her vocation. The following passage is from her book, *Sex Secrets of Escorts: Tips from a Pro*:

> I see myself as a sexual, spiritual creature. I envision sex as a creative force, a physical manifestation of the spiritual force of love, and the very core essence of life. Pleasure is part of spiritual reality, not a distraction from it. . . . if life is sacred simply because it is life, then sex is sacred as well—simply because it is sex.[11] . . . Claiming our birth-right as goddesses is a very powerful and life-changing act. In doing so, we affirm our central role in history as well as our creative influence over the future.[12]

As Paris stressed, a reconsideration of goddess-centered attitudes and sexual practices is not a wish to relive the past or a directive to enact it in the way that Monet chose to do; rather, it constitutes an intention to reinvigorate important val-ues from which we have become disconnected.

THE GODDESSES AND GODS AT PLAY

A revaluing of the teachings of Aphrodite and the Divine Feminine, especially regarding the importance of balancing

feminine with masculine energies, also illuminates the transformative potential of love and sex. To enter fully into either
or both of these experiences necessarily involves giving ourselves over to unconscious forces or what we might view
as the "play" of the unacknowledged deities residing in our
psyches. Understanding the nature of that play can give shape
and meaning to our lives and help us make sense of major
and mysterious life events. But to do so, we must confront an
inner paradox.

When divine powers are at work in our lives, especially in our
encounters with others, we may feel we are at the mercy of forces
so much bigger than ourselves that we have little choice over our
desires and behaviors. As a consequence, we may act in ways that
surprise those around us and even ourselves. We must always
remember, though, that we do have at least a modicum of choice
as to whether and how much we surrender to such forces. If we
choose to move forward consciously or, at least, as consciously
as possible, we invite in the possibility of growth, though admit-
tedly, the price of that growth may be high.

Analytical psychologist Eleanor Bertine's vivid description
of the potentially transformative experience of passionate love
gives a good sense of its impact. She described this dynamic as
it occurs between a man and a woman, but it could also occur
between individuals of the same sex:

> In any relation between a man and a woman that
> touches the deeper levels, the conscious interchange
> between them is accompanied by an obligato from

the archetypal world which offers them a chance to be lifted out of their banal and limited selves and to participate in the fateful experience of life's august suprapersonal powers—powers which have always been worshipped, or placated, as gods. . . . These are the experiences of love, of death, and of poetry. . . . Not the love of friendship where human companionship plays the leading role; but the love in passion, where a nonpersonal daemonic factor takes possession, raising the participants to a level of intensity beyond that of their daily lives.[13]

Even if you were never taught to deeply honor your own sexuality or consciously experienced its sacred and transcendent aspect, you may have been touched by divine energies in the realms of love and sex without being fully aware of it.

To explore that possibility, start by bringing to mind a personal memory of seduction. Perhaps you were the seducer or the seduced. Whichever role you played, were you lucky enough to have been swept away in love beyond the bounds of what seemed rational or sensible? Think of a time when your imagination and your behavior felt driven by irresistible energies that seemed greater than yourself. Most people have had this experience at least once in their lives, and if not, they probably wish they had.

Sometimes alcohol or other substances help fuel our abandon, but often it is the force of the experience itself and how our imaginations have been activated that leads us to venture into the unknown. Many people have found the ancient wisdom of Tantra to be helpful in integrating sex, body, mind, and spirit, as well as unifying feminine and masculine energies within themselves. Margot Anand is one author and teacher who has explored this subject extensively through numerous publications and workshops.[14]

[Eroticism] is the poetry of the body, the testimony of the senses. Like a poem, it is not linear, it meanders and twists back on itself, shows us what we do not see with our eyes, but in the eyes of our spirit. Eroticism reveals us to another world, inside this world. The senses become servants of the imagination, and let us see the invisible and hear the inaudible.

—OCTAVIO PAZ, *The Double Flame: Love and Eroticism*

When it comes to romantic love and seduction, Aphrodite reigns supreme in the Greek pantheon, but she is joined in her authority over love's passionate sexual expression by three other gods: her son Eros; Dionysus, God of Wine and Ecstasy; and Ares, God of War. The psychic activity of each of these gods in our lives—which is dependent on our conscious and unconscious relationships to the energies they represent—profoundly affects our experiences of love and sex. I discussed aspects of Eros's role in setting the stage for love and sexual expression earlier. The roles of Dionysus and Ares in these arenas similarly deserve some attention.

When Dionysus makes his presence known in intimate encounters, he is usually fairly easy to recognize. Dionysus is about intensity, excitement, and freedom, and his influence can be found in acts of rebellion and liberation from the demands of society and one's personal ego, including ecstatic sexual encounters. Dionysian energy is related to the wildness of nature and can be extremely powerful and potentially spiritually transformative, but too much of it can result in decadence.

Ares's presence also introduces intensity into sexual relationships, but it is of a very different type. Like Dionysus, Ares's energy is emotional and impulsive, but unlike Dionysus, who was close to the mystical and feminine worlds, Ares embodies aggressiveness, reactivity, and raw masculinity. Ares is also associated with courage and loyalty, but it was his uncontrolled and combative nature that led to him being disliked and rejected by most other Olympians, including his parents Hera and Zeus. Those same negative personality aspects are problematic for real-life individuals if they are not tempered by maturity and self-restraint. On the positive side, Ares's physicality, strong emotions, and ability to immerse himself in his immediate experience can add compelling lustiness and passion to intimate relationships.

Both Dionysus and Ares deserve a place beside Aphrodite in the realm of sexuality, and there can be much satisfaction in a primarily Dionysian or Arean experience of lovemaking. At the same time, Aphrodisian sensibilities need not be completely excluded from such experiences. Aphrodite's more refined approach to sensuality and gentler cultivation of desire can provide balance to the frenzy of a Dionysian or the aggressiveness of an Arean encounter.

What matters most is that lovers are compatible when it comes to their erotic desires and expressions. Given that Aphrodite is orientated toward making her desires and needs known, we can presume that she sought compatibility in all her sexual liaisons (even when that compatibility was expressed in mutual volatility), including her brief affair with Dionysus and her lengthy relationship with Ares.

The most rewarding sexual encounters also occur when each participant has acquired erotic knowledge of the other—a multifaceted awareness that enables each person to sense when to take what approach in the service of love and pleasure. This is not about developing a repertoire of sexual techniques, however broad or skillfully applied. Instead, it refers to paying keen attention to the mood, desires, and preferences of one's lover, and of course, those of one's own self. Such knowledge can only be attained through personal experience and reflection.

We have been bombarded over the years with verbal, visual, and pharmaceutical prescriptions of how we are all supposed to think, feel, look, act, and respond in even the most intimate of encounters. For most people, those imperatives have been intimidating, demoralizing, depersonalizing, and soul-destroying. The corrective is to actively disengage from any cultural elements that get in the way of experiencing true pleasure, passion, and vitality, whether that be sexual or otherwise.

Instead, choose to engage your courage, curiosity, and imagination in service to inviting these experiences into your life. And remember that each act of love-making is, at some level, a reenactment of an archetypal union of divine energies. To the degree that each partner is aware of this truth, they activate the potential to transcend their personal ego needs. Out of that transcendence, a truly sacred experience can arise. Jungian author M. Esther Harding stressed the importance of giving ourselves over to suprapersonal values:

> The most precious things of life do not belong to us personally. In our most intimate acts, our most secret moments, we are *lived* by Life. . . . our little personal egos must be surpassed; only so we can take our place in the stream of life . . . For when two people experience each other unmasked—in stark reality—emotional energy which has had its counterpart in the past only in religious experience is in modern times released and made available for human development.[15]

None of the previous discussion about the potential sanctity and transcendent power of sex or about Aphrodite's sensitive and graceful nature is meant to give the impression that her energy is in any way devoid of lightness or humor. In fact, among the many descriptors the Greeks gave to this goddess were "Smile-Loving" and "Laughter-Loving." Remember, she values pleasure, and that naturally includes the simple pleasure of having fun. C. S. Lewis provided a nice summary of the importance of this aspect of Aphrodite-Venus:

We must not be totally serious about Venus. Indeed we can't be totally serious without doing violence to our humanity. It is not for nothing that every language and literature in the world is full of jokes about sex . . . Banish play and laughter from the bed of love and you may let in a false goddess . . . The mass of the people are perfectly right in their conviction that Venus is a partly comic spirit. We are under no obligation at all to sing all our love-duets in the throbbing, world-without-end, heart-breaking manner of Tristan and Isolde; let us often sing like Papageno and Papagena instead.[16]

How, then, can you as an individual utilize the wisdom of Aphrodite to enhance eroticism and enlightened sexual experiences in your own life? Begin by appreciating the miracle of your own body and treat it, as well as your heart and your feelings, with loving care. This is as true for those who do not have sexual partners as for those who do. Being single need not preclude anyone from living a life rich in beauty and sensuality. I explore this topic in more depth in Chapter 8 ("Love, Beauty, and the Senses").

For those who are sexually active, be sure to only choose partners who will also appreciate and treat with care your body and heart, who will support your values, who will respectfully and joyfully attend to your senses and preferences, and who will laugh along with you when love and sex take a comical turn. Of course, treat your partners with the same sensitivity with which you wish to be treated. And when you are so inclined, take the time to allow the delicious experience of seduction to unfold.

The woman we recognize as Cleopatra, Queen of Egypt (c. 69–10 BCE), is a wonderful though highly exceptional example of someone who lived a life rich in sensuality, immersed in the mysteries of Aphrodite. The Cleopatra most of us have heard of is more accurately identified as the Ptolemaic queen Cleopatra VII who genealogists estimate was three-quarters Greek and only one-quarter Egyptian. (The Ptolemies were Macedonian Greeks.) But as a designated Egyptian queen, she considered herself—and was considered by others—to be the living incarnation of Isis, the goddess named Aphrodite, Venus, or Astarte in other regions of the Mediterranean. Cleopatra is known to have used her beauty and her seductive skills to political as well as personal advantage, but history has done her a major disservice by understating other strengths such as her considerable military, administrative, and financial acumen. Instead, emphasis has been placed on her notably lavish lifestyle and spirited love life.

One of many examples of the sensuous style in which Cleopatra lived was her extravagant use of perfume. She was not unique in Egypt in her love of perfume—the Egyptians were masterful in their use of aromatics—but she was, in author Diane Ackerman's words, its "quintessential devotee." Here is Ackerman's description of how Cleopatra received her lover, the Roman general Mark Antony:

> [Her] cedarwood ship . . . had perfumed sails; incense burners ringed her throne, and she herself was scented from head to toe . . . She anointed her hands with *kyphi*, which contained oil of roses, crocus, and violets; she scented her feet with *aegyptium*,

a lotion of almond oil, honey, cinnamon, orange blossoms, and henna. The walls were an aviary of roses secured by nets, and her regally perfumed presence arrived before her, like a kind of calling card in the scent-drenched wind.[17]

Keeping in mind that Cleopatra was a queen, a powerful and sometimes ruthless ruler, and phenomenally wealthy, it is an understatement to say that she is hardly a realistic role model for our time. But she was a fascinating woman who pushed the boundaries of the role that fate delivered her, and she did so while also honoring her divine feminine nature. We may not choose to carpet our bedrooms with a foot-and-a-half of rose petals as did Cleopatra when she invited in Mark Antony, but perhaps we can use that image and her devotion to sensuality as inspiration to create environments that will entice our own inner Aphrodite to emerge.

Chapter 6

Let's Talk About Beauty

A thing of beauty is a joy forever:

Its loveliness increases; it will never

Pass into nothingness; but still will keep

A bower quiet for us, and a sleep

Full of sweet dreams, and health, and quiet breathing.

—JOHN KEATS, "ENDYMION"

In 1981 the American writer Raymond Carver published a short story called "What We Talk About When We Talk About Love."[1] With respect to its creator, I will borrow from his phraseology: What do we talk about when we talk about beauty? The answer is when we talk about beauty, as with love, we talk about many different things.

Beauty, alongside love, is one of Aphrodite's great realms of influence, and among the Greek deities, it belongs to her alone. Although poetry and art, two expressions of beauty, are under Athena's and Apollo's divine rulerships, only Aphrodite presides over beauty's full domain. However, because Aphrodite's physical beauty has been so celebrated over the ages, she is often associated solely with female attractiveness and sexual allure rather than with beauty in a larger sense. In this chapter, as I explore the nature and impact of beauty in our lives, it is important to remember that Aphrodite's life-affirming spirit infuses all manifestations of beauty, natural or man-made.

WHAT BEAUTY MAY BE

Research on the topic of beauty delivers a wide range of opinions about what beauty is and what makes something beautiful. It is a complex and controversial issue, and many theorists who write about beauty avoid giving a precise definition of the term, choosing instead to concentrate on what makes for a valid assessment of beauty or provide analyses of how beauty affects us. I am also going to step gingerly around defining beauty and present a few of the perspectives I have come across that are relevant to an exploration of how beauty can serve as a catalyst for transformation.

Look up "beauty" in any dictionary and you will likely find a definition similar to *Merriam-Webster*'s: "the quality or aggregate of qualities in a person or thing that gives pleasure to the senses or pleasurably exalts the mind or spirit."[2] To what extent our personal assessments of the "quality or aggregate of qualities" we deem beautiful are influenced by social and cultural factors is an issue that has been debated for thousands of years.

Common associations with the word beauty in Western

culture are truth, goodness, and morality. The idea that beauty is a value to be equated with truth and goodness is an ancient one with roots in the writings of the Hellenistic philosophers Plato and Plotinus, as well as in the theological vision of Saint Thomas Aquinas. Many readers will be familiar with the poet John Keats's 1819 assertion in "Ode on a Grecian Urn": "Beauty is truth, truth beauty—that is all/Ye know on earth, and all ye need to know."[3] Keats's affirmation is wonderfully succinct but elusive. Still, as the aesthetics scholar Roger Scruton pointed out, Keats's lines capture an important element of the relationship between beauty and truth which speaks to the affective power of beauty:

> Keats's vision of the Grecian urn . . . arises from a lingering glance at a vanished world. But it records a common experience. Our favorite works of art seem to guide us to the truth of the human condition and, by presenting completed instances of human actions and passions, freed from the contingencies of everyday life, to show the worthwhileness of being.[4]

Scruton's comment supports his general argument that beauty is a real and universal value anchored in our rational nature and that beauty plays an indispensable part in shaping humans' perception of the world.

The idea that beauty is an objective universally experienced quality of something—that is, beauty is located in an object itself or in its qualities—prevailed until the eighteenth century. At that time, prominent philosophers such as Immanuel

Kant and David Hume promoted the contrary idea that beauty is primarily subjective. Kant stated that beauty has a fundamentally subjective nature and that every judgment of beauty is based on personal experience, which would necessarily vary between individuals. Hume asserted that: "Beauty is no quality in things themselves: It exists merely in the mind which contemplates them; and each mind perceives a different beauty. One person may even perceive deformity, where another is sensible of beauty; and every individual ought to acquiesce to his own sentiment, without pretending to regulate those of others."[5]

Over time, Kant, Hume, and others of like mind modified their stance that beauty is always subjective and proposed that, in some circumstances, it can also be an objective experience. One example is aesthetic taste, which can be understood to be both subjective and objective because there can be both individual and cultural judgments about what is "good" or "bad" taste.

Nevertheless, the idea that beauty is subjective to the observer has retained its influence over hundreds of years, and most everyone nowadays, without necessarily knowing anything about the history of aesthetics, is familiar with the sentiment that "beauty is in the eye of the beholder." This familiar saying has ancient origins. According to etymologists, a version of it first appeared in Greek in the third century BCE but did not appear in written English until the nineteenth century. In the intervening years, writers as diverse as William Shakespeare and Benjamin Franklin expressed similar thoughts, but it is the author Margaret Hungerford who is credited with coining the precise phrase "beauty is in the eye of the beholder" when she included it in her 1878 novel *Molly Bawn*.

Deliberations about the nature and role of beauty in our lives have continued to the present day. The following are three contemporary examples of the types of discussions taking place in the public arena.

The first is philosopher Denis Dutton's "A Darwinian Theory of Beauty," which he presented in 2010 in a popular and provocative TED Talk. Dutton's thesis was that our appreciation of beauty reflects universal cross-cultural aesthetics and values that have deep evolutionary roots. He esteemed these as "a gift handed down from the intelligent skills and rich emotional lives of our most ancient ancestors."[6] Dutton identified three common elements in anything we find beautiful: that it has a shape or features that we instinctively like because they are based on natural forms, that it be fit for purpose, and that it be well executed whatever its function—whether it be a stone tool or a piece of art or music.

The second example is designer Richard Seymour's 2011 TED Talk on "How Beauty Feels." Like Dutton, Seymour highlighted the relationship between our perception of beauty and our appreciation of skilled performance. However, unlike Dutton, he focused on how our personal emotional responses, rather than universally inherited ones, shape that perception. Seymour emphasized that any emotional response to a phenomenon affecting the senses can be mediated by multiple factors, including information attained personally before or after exposure to that phenomenon, such as knowledge of its context or complexity, which will affect our feelings about it. In his opinion, "Beauty is in the limbic system of the beholder."[7]

A third exploration of beauty was presented in 2006 by Crispin Sartwell, a philosopher specializing in aesthetics. In *Six Names for Beauty*, Sartwell reflected on the challenge of defining beauty, suggested that it should not be and perhaps cannot be defined, and explored how varying cultural perspectives influence people's experiences of it. The six words he highlighted are: "beauty" (English), meaning "the object of longing"; *yapha* (Hebrew), meaning "glow or bloom"; *sundara* (Sanskrit), meaning "whole or holy"; *kalon* (Greek), meaning "idea or ideal"; *wabi-sabi* (Japanese), meaning "humility or imperfection"; and *hozho* (Navajo), meaning "health or harmony." While acknowledging the differences between these perspectives, Sartwell also identified in them a shared relationship to spirit: "Beauty is fundamentally connected to spirit in every culture, and every religion expresses its spirituality in some of its most exquisitely made objects, which are offered to God, or to the people as a way to achieve contact with God."[8]

EXALTATION OF THE SPIRIT

All three of these conceptualizations in some way link beauty to "the pleasurable exaltation of our minds and spirits" or, expressed alternatively, "the pleasurable exaltation of our level of consciousness." Indeed, because of beauty's power to exalt us, the pursuit and promotion of beauty can be considered a crucial aspect of living a good life. John-Mark Miravalle, a Christian scholar, held a similar view:

> Beauty is like happiness, love, understanding—it is what the human person was made for. Experiencing beauty is itself a kind of mix of love, happiness, and understanding. In any case, an orientation toward beauty is intrinsic to our nature. Attaining beauty is part of our purpose. And since it is everyone's responsibility to fulfill his purpose, beauty is everybody's moral responsibility.[9]

None of the myths about Aphrodite suggest that the Goddess was at all concerned with "moral responsibility," at least by collective standards, but Miravalle's main point is still consistent with Aphrodite's teachings. Aphrodite embodies the idea that "an orientation toward beauty" is part of our nature and that attaining it is part of our purpose. In the active honoring of beauty, we honor her and the Divine Feminine.

A similar ethical and spiritual perspective is reflected in the Navajo's—or Diné's—use of the word *hozho*. *Hozho* is difficult to translate into English, but it is worth contemplating because it offers a broad conceptualization of beauty that non-Navajo people could benefit from embracing. For the Navajo, beauty is more than an aesthetic concept. The experience of beauty, as reflected in *hozho*, is integral to their values and way of life. According to anthropologist Clyde Kluckhohn, *hozho*:

> . . . is probably the central idea in Navajo religious thinking. It occurs in the names of two important

ceremonials (Blessing Way and Beauty Way) and is frequently repeated in almost all prayers and songs. In various contexts it is best translated as "beautiful," "harmonious," "good," "blessed," "pleasant,"and "satisfying.". . . the difficulty with translation primarily reflects the poverty of English in terms that simultaneously have moral and esthetic meaning.[10]

Navajo ceremonies are typically multifaceted and vary in their focus and details, but all are meant to help restore and maintain harmony within the individual, the community, and the natural world.

Two scientific perspectives are also relevant to an understanding of how beauty can exalt us. The first is the principle that everything has an energetic frequency and that these frequencies vary across feelings, mindsets, and experiences. For instance, "negative" emotions such as despair or fear are deemed by researchers to vibrate at a lower frequency than "positive" emotions such as hope or serenity. But it is not only humans or human experiences that emit frequencies.

According to physicists, all objects or phenomena have a natural frequency or set of frequencies at which they vibrate. Since we almost universally consider encounters with beauty to be positive and life-affirming, we can assume that anything of beauty emits a high vibrational frequency level regardless of its context. Given that premise, if we resonate (that is, we synchronize vibrationally) with any object or phenomenon we assess as beautiful, we stand to benefit in multiple ways—emotionally, mentally, spiritually, and physically—even if our perception of that object or phenomenon's beauty is subtle or unconscious.

A second scientific perspective is provided by the emerging field of neuroaesthetics, which examines the intersection of psychological aesthetics, biological mechanisms, and human evolution. The term "neuroaesthetics" originated with neurobiologist Semir Zeki in 1999 and is defined as the scientific study of the neural bases for the contemplation and creation of a work of art.

According to researcher Susan Magsamen, aesthetic experiences and the arts are hard-wired in all of us. They affect profound positive changes in our thoughts, emotions, and actions and are linked to our survival by helping us communicate and connect. In her view, "Identifying the systems and brain mechanisms that respond to the arts is like finding a map to a hidden treasure. Cutting-edge brain research is revealing in greater detail how aesthetic experiences enter the brain through the portal of the senses and—whether we're aware of it or not—profoundly impact our biological circuitry."[11]

Notably, even as this field of inquiry continues to grow, some critics have objected to its attempts to reduce aesthetic experiences to a set of physical or neurological laws. They have questioned not only the limits of the theories that have so far been proposed about how the brain processes aesthetic information but also the validity of the methodology used in many of the studies.[12]

It was Stendhal who offered the most crystalline expression of the intimate affiliation between visual taste and our values when he wrote, "Beauty is the promise of happiness." His aphorism has the virtue of differentiating our love of beauty from an academic preoccupation with aesthetics, and integrating it instead with the qualities we need to prosper as whole human beings. If the search for happiness is the underlying quest of our lives, it seems only natural that it should simultaneously be the essential theme to which beauty alludes.... What we seek at the deepest level, is inwardly to resemble, rather than physically to possess the objects and places that touch us through their beauty.

—ALAIN DE BOTTON, *The Architecture of Happiness*

BEAUTY IN ANCIENT GREECE

Historians disagree as to whether or not the ancient Greeks thought of beauty in the same way we do now or even if they had a word for beauty that is equivalent to our modern use of the term, multifaceted though our own usage may be. Still, that civilization is acknowledged by many as having made a seminal contribution to the concept of beauty. The author David Konstan credited the Greeks with inventing beauty, which he called "Western civilization's biggest idea."[13] He proposed that for them, beauty could not be separated from eros or passionate desire—a relationship reflected in the word *kállos*. The close association of the two terms explains why *kállos* was used in Greek texts more often to describe Aphrodite than other goddesses such as Athena and Artemis, who do not emanate sensuality and stimulate sexual desire as does Aphrodite.

Certainly, the integration of beauty and desire was reflected in ancient Grecian practices designed to enhance one's physical beauty. These practices were extensive, especially for women, though men also strove to attain an ideal image. Beauty was seen to be not only a physical attribute but also a spiritual one—a divine gift—and was highlighted in representations and stories of the deities, especially Aphrodite, who was regarded as the ultimate model of feminine beauty. Some of those stories exalt beauty, and some also point to its dark power to incite jealousy, disputes, and even violence as discussed in earlier chapters.

One famous myth illustrating the complexity of beauty's power is "The Judgment of Paris," which features a beauty contest that is said to have started a war. In that myth, Eris, the Goddess of Discord, discovered she had not been invited to the wedding of Peleus and Thetis, but she turned up anyway and with a gift in hand: a Golden Apple inscribed with the words "For the Fairest." An argument ensued among the Goddesses Aphrodite, Athena, and Hera as to which one of them deserved the prize. To resolve the conflict, the three of them agreed that Paris, the Prince of Troy, would make the decision.

Each goddess offered Paris a bribe. Athena offered wisdom, Hera offered power, and Aphrodite offered the hand of Helen, the most beautiful of mortal women. Aphrodite then presented herself to Paris in all her naked glory, and he immediately awarded her the Golden Apple. In turn, she arranged for him to abduct Helen who was (inconveniently) already married to King Menelaus of Sparta. That abduction led to Menelaus launching a thousand ships to retrieve Helen, thus beginning the Trojan War.[14]

A BEAUTIFUL AND GOLDEN NUMBER

Beauty can be found in every sphere of life, and those who are sensitive to the beauty of mathematics will know that when the ratio between two differing line segments equals (approximately) 1.618, it is called the "golden proportion" or "golden ratio." That ratio, represented by the Greek letter *phi* (Φ), has many unique mathematical properties and is considered an integral part of sacred geometry.

An appreciation of the golden ratio is pertinent to a comprehensive understanding of beauty because its presence in geometrical and other contexts is known to be aesthetically pleasing. It is also easy to identify once you know what to look for. The presence of the golden ratio is abundant in nature and can be found in the physical forms and markings of plants, animals, and humans (from the structure of human DNA to the facial proportions we find attractive), as well as in the larger cosmos (where we see the mathematical relationships amongst the components of the solar system). It has also been purposely used by artists and artisans throughout history and is present in the compositions of many classical and modern artworks, graphic and product designs, photos, videos, and architecture, and even (some say) in the recurrent patterns of the stock and currency markets.

Wherever it appears, the golden ratio affects us psychologically and emotionally. We universally experience its presence as harmonious and beautiful in its proportions, experiences that are in full alignment with the values of Aphrodite and the Divine Feminine. This is relevant both on a spiritual and a practical level. If the contemplation of the divine ratio brings harmony and beauty into our lives, even unconsciously, how can we then intentionally give greater attention to those environments, objects, and natural elements that reflect its proportions?

Apropos to a discussion of Aphrodite-Venus, Gary B. Meisner, in his book *The Golden Ratio: The Divine Beauty of Mathematics*, presented a detailed analysis of how several key elements of Sandro Botticelli's painting *The Birth of Venus* are positioned according to golden ratio principles. The painting was considered revolutionary when it was created in the late 1480s due to its depiction of nudity and the fact that it was meant to be displayed over a marriage bed, a bold reference at the time to sensuality and desire. There are many reasons why this artwork has continued to be such a focus of attention and so greatly admired over the centuries. That it lovingly portrays the splendor of Venus's arrival into the world is one reason, and that this portrayal is in accordance with the golden ratio is undoubtedly another.

Botticelli's use of the golden ratio is especially impressive because he applied his knowledge of this subject decades before the publishing in 1509 of Luca Pacioli's influential book *De Divina Proportione*, which connected mathematics to art and architecture and explored the historical presence and uses of phi. Here is a short excerpt from Meisner's analysis of the overall proportions of Botticelli's masterpiece:

> The first clue is found in the dimensions of the canvas itself, which is 67.9 X 109.6 inches (172.5 X 278.5 cm). The ratio of the width to the height is thus 1.6168, a variance of only 0.08 percent from the golden ratio of 1.618. To put in perspective, for the canvas to have been an exact golden ratio, the height of the canvas would need to be reduced by less than one twentieth of an inch! The width of the painting at 109.6 inches (278 cm) seems somewhat arbitrary. That is, until one realizes that the units of measure were not standardized in this era . . . it is quite reasonable to conclude that Botticelli's intent here was to begin this great work of art with the perfection of the golden ratio.[15]

When considering the golden ratio, whether in artworks or elsewhere, it is helpful to remember that harmony and beauty are not the same as symmetry, though some symmetrical objects or elements may indeed seem harmonious and beautiful to us. We often think we see perfect symmetry in nature when it is not actually there. Many small natural elements, such as flowers or other plants, can appear to be symmetrical, but what we are really seeing are expressions of the Fibonacci sequence—a set of numbers from classical mathematics in which each number is the sum of the last two numbers, starting with 0 and 1.

The Fibonacci sequence is closely linked to the golden ratio, and its distinctive spiral shape—think of the spiral pattern of a nautilus shell—is ubiquitous in nature. It also has many practical and theoretical applications in areas such as mathematics, computer science, and financial forecasting. Examples of the Fibonacci sequence in nature range from the very small (rows of seeds or the shape of a tiny animal's curling tail) to very big (large objects or events viewed from a distance, such as the shape of hurricanes or galaxies).

Those who contemplate the beauty of the earth find reserves of strength that will endure as long as life lasts. There is something infinitely healing in the repeated refrains of nature—the assurance that dawn comes after night, and spring after winter.

—RACHEL CARSON, *The Sense of Wonder*

BEAUTY'S VARIED PRESENCE

Imperfection, as well as asymmetry, can also create or enhance our experience of harmony and beauty. The Japanese concept of *wabi-sabi* is an excellent illustration of this. *Wabi* is best translated as "poverty," not in a negative sense, but as related to humility, asymmetry, and imperfection. *Sabi* means "loneliness" in the sense of aloneness and spareness. In Crispin Sartwell's words: "Wabi-sabi is an aesthetic of poverty and loneliness, imperfection and austerity, affirmation and melancholy. [It is] the beauty of the withered, weathered, tarnished, scarred, intimate, coarse, earthly, evanescent, tentative, ephemeral."[16]

We can find *wabi-sabi* in any object or creation that reflects that aesthetic: a roughly glazed bowl, a silver vase left intentionally tarnished, a weather-beaten wooden box, or well-worn leather shoes with the patina of age. *Wabi-sabi* can also be found in nature, particularly in fall and winter in the northern hemisphere when the trees are stripped bare of leaves, and we are able to observe the starkness and transformative decay of the natural world.

As beautiful as the *wabi-sabi* aesthetic may be, it is only partially in alignment with an Aphrodisian approach to beauty. What the two expressions have in common is a valuing of the ephemeral, especially the ephemeral aspect of the natural world. Both emphasize the beauty and the beautification of the impermanent. As the myth of Aphrodite and Adonis reminds us, nothing on this earth lasts forever, though there is always the prospect of rebirth. To fully embrace that truth is to commit to inviting beauty, love, sensuousness, and refinement into all aspects of our lives *in the present moment*.

But where a *wabi-sabi*–influenced approach to beauty differs from an Aphrodisian one is in the former's valuing of not just what is old but what is decaying. *Wabi-sabi's* seasons are fall and winter, whereas Aphrodite's season is spring, when nature comes to life again and, as Alfred Tennyson wrote, "a young man's fancy lightly turns to thoughts of love."[17]

Of course, spring can do the same for young women, and for older men and women too. An Aphrodisian sensibility is not restricted to the young. Men and women of any age are free to adopt attitudes and practices that bring experiences of freshness and renewal into their lives in any ways that are personally meaningful. They can also choose to recognize and celebrate not only the many instances of beauty that are external to them in the world but also their own inner and outer beauty. Granted, this is not always easy in a society that is youth-obsessed, especially regarding standards of physical attractiveness for women, but it is possible if we are willing to expand our vision and our appreciation of what constitutes true beauty.

Love Is Ageless—A Memory Photograph

I used to work next door to a harborside public market, and I liked to go there just as it was waking up. The coffee stalls would open first to serve the vendors and a few people like me who wanted to get an early start to the day. One summer morning, I bought a coffee and took a seat with a view of the water. The only other patrons in the public area were an elderly couple at a table a little distance from me and closer to the window. I chose to watch them—discreetly—instead of the boats as I would usually do.

It was their apparent delight in being together that captured my attention. They smiled and laughed and leaned in toward one another conspiratorially. There was no telling if this was the first morning they were spending together or another one of thousands. Other than their happy demeanor, nothing about their appearance was especially noteworthy except I remember that they both had hair as white as their coffee cups and the woman's slippers glowed golden in a shaft of sunlight.

OUR LONGING FOR BEAUTY

In whatever form beauty presents itself to us, and however individual our evaluations of it may be, we will always seek out beauty because we need the emotional, spiritual, and—according to neuroaestheticists—biological sustenance it provides. The writer and poet John O'Donohue addressed our deep longing for beauty:

> The human soul is hungry for beauty: we seek it everywhere—in landscape, music, art, clothes, furniture, gardening, companionship, love, religion, and in ourselves. No one would desire not to be beautiful. When we experience the Beautiful there is a sense of homecoming. Some of our most wonderful memories are of beautiful places where we felt immediately at home. We feel most alive in the presence of the Beautiful for it meets the needs of our soul. For a while the strains of struggle and endurance are relieved and our frailty is illuminated by a different light in which we come to glimpse behind the shudder of appearances the sure form of things. In the experience of beauty we awaken and surrender in the same act. Beauty brings a sense of completion and sureness. Without any of the usual calculation, we can slip into the Beautiful with the same ease as we slip into the seamless embrace of water; something ancient within us already trusts that this embrace will hold us.[18]

In light of O'Donohue's sentiments, it is disheartening to realize how often people mitigate their experience of beauty by distancing themselves from it, intentionally or unintentionally, through the use of electronic filters. Can we really "slip into the Beautiful" when we, as is now commonly done, view landscapes, flowers, natural wonders, or even deeply personal and meaningful events—from births and funerals to weddings and other celebratory gatherings—primarily through the lens of a mobile phone camera? I am sure Beauty would rather us pay full, unmediated attention to its presence and splendor.

The Eyes of Beholders

As I was writing this book, I chanced upon a charming example of just how singular our notions of beauty can be. By virtue of YouTube's algorithm, I was led to the first day of a week-long video marathon of lessons by Bob Ross, the American painter and art instructor best known for hosting a televised series called *The Joy of Painting*. The original series ran from 1983 to 1994 and has been replayed many times on television and the internet. Ross died in 1995, but he continues to have a large following. Some fans appear to view him solely through an ironic lens, but others seem genuinely respectful of both the man and his work.

I checked in on the marathon from time to time over the week of its broadcast. Not only did I enjoy rekindling my own fond memories of *The Joy of Painting* but I also was fascinated by the conversations in the live chat. It struck me that it was a wonderful example of the subjective nature of beauty. Some viewers—many of whom shared how many consecutive hours they had been watching—playfully posted bets on the chances of yet another wood cabin appearing in one of Ross's idyllic mountain scenes or mimicked his famous catchphrase about creating "happy little clouds/trees/accidents" in his paintings.

continued

A subgroup of those viewers emphasized how "chill" they felt watching his videos and praised the ASMR quality of his voice. (ASMR stands for Autonomous Sensory Meridian Response, a pleasant bodily tingling sensation that some people experience in response to stimuli such as soft whispering, repetitive gentle touch, or light patterns. ASMR sensations usually evoke feelings of relaxation, calm, and well-being.) Other viewers focused on his artistic approach; several of those said they found it to be formulaic but admired his use of technique or color choices.

A final smaller group of viewers seemed to express sincere admiration for his finished paintings. Someone in that last group said that Ross was able to capture "unseen beauty," another declared a painting of a vivid sunset to be a "masterpiece," and still another shared a touching memory stirred by that same image: "I remember sunset skies like that at auntie's, the adults sitting on the porch drinking fresh made lemonade and talking about the old days, us kids in the backyard chasing fireflies."

That last comment led me to ponder Bob Ross's legacy. Whether or not any particular viewer deems his paintings to be aesthetically beautiful, surely there is beauty to be found in the longstanding impact of his genial spirit, the calming effect of his uniquely mesmerizing delivery, the obvious love he took in his work, and the encouragement he gave others.

The livestream ended after a week, but as of this writing, there are still many online videos available of his classes, and I would bet they will remain popular for a very long time. Wherever Bob Ross is, I imagine he is smiling serenely down on his fans and commenting with his familiar warmth, "Happy little people!"

Chapter 7

Beauty's Opposition

Nothing is more important than that you see and love the beauty
that is right in front of you or else you will have no defense against
the ugliness that will hem you in and come at you in so many ways.

—NEAL STEPHENSON, *Anathem*

T he most obvious answer to the question of what opposes
beauty is to say it is whatever we judge as ugly. Or as the
poet Plotinus (c. 204–270 CE) defined it, ugly is that which
makes the soul "shrink within itself, denies the thing, turns
away from it, resentful and alienated from it."[1] Ugliness has
always existed as the antithesis to beauty, and like beauty, it can
elicit strong reactions—though usually of an opposite nature.

But despite its inevitable presence in our lives, historical
and contemporary explorations of ugliness are much fewer in
number than those that have addressed the subject of beauty.
Perhaps philosophers and aesthetic scholars have preferred to

turn away, just as most of us do, from dwelling on a phenom-enon that can elicit such intensely uncomfortable feelings.

That said, we do know that our perception of ugliness, like our perception of beauty, may have personal, cultural, and evolutionary components, and the relationship between ugliness and beauty for any individual may be complex. As the writer Umberto Eco noted, we can sometimes be fascinated and seduced by the passionate response that ugliness evokes in us, even as we are repelled by our encounters with it. Furthermore, he stated: "Contrary to Plato who said that the representation of ugliness should be avoided, from Aristotle onwards it has been admitted in all periods that even the ugliness in life can be beautifully portrayed, and that it actually serves to make beauty stand out or to support a certain moral theory."[2]

That may be so, but there is evidence all around us that our manmade world has become increasingly and distressingly ugly in the eyes, as well as the other senses, of a great many of us. And just as we can experience salutary psychological effects when we encounter beauty in our environment—such as through the harmonious proportions of the golden ratio—we can experience negative effects when we are confronted with sensory stimuli that we find unpleasant or unharmonious. These can leave us feeling disturbed, depressed, and anxious. (A friend and I often joke about having a "visual allergy" to anything we find ugly.)

Our manmade world, especially as it is displayed in our urban environments, is now widely experienced as not only having become less beautiful over time but also less human-friendly. This unfortunate regression in standards of beauty in our towns and cities is often attributed simply to a lack of imagination on the part of designers or financial constraints on the part of builders. These may be important factors in any particular instance, but there are also other more general influences at work that have driven this change.

Nowadays, whether we like it or not, we are stuck with one form or another of advanced technology and we have got to make it work safely and efficiently: this involves, among other things, the intelligent application of structural theory. However, man does not live by safety and efficiency alone, and we have to face the fact that, visually, the world is becoming an increasingly depressing place. It is not, perhaps, so much the occurrence of what might be described as "active ugliness" as the prevalence of the dull and the commonplace. Far too seldom is the heart rejoiced or does one feel any better or happier for looking at the works of modern man. Yet most of the artefacts of the eighteenth century, even quite humble and trivial ones, seem to many of us to be at least pleasing and sometimes incomparably beautiful. To that extent people—all people—in the eighteenth century lived richer lives than most of us do today. This is reflected in the prices we pay nowadays for period houses and antiques. A society which was more creative and self-confident would not feel quite so strong a nostalgia for its great-grandfathers' buildings and household looks.

—J. E. GORDON, *Structures:*
Or Why Things Don't Fall Down

ARCHITECTURE

Consider the typical layout of modern towns and cities where most of the streets and buildings are set up in a grid pattern reminiscent of the layout of a computer circuit board and designed primarily for the efficient movement of vehicles. The streets no longer encourage organic exploration as do many of those constructed in earlier times. Anyone who has visited the old section of a pre-industrial European town knows that the typically narrow winding streets invite meandering and interaction with others.

In most urban centers in the West, the majority of people now live and work in buildings that are not only aesthetically unappealing but, due to their floor plans, lead to experiences of isolation among their inhabitants. This is the case even in—and often especially in—buildings that are designed to efficiently house large numbers of people. Also, in such environments, there is frequently little to no access provided for people to go outdoors.

We know instinctively—and research bears this out—that we are nourished physically and emotionally by spending time outside and in nature, but in many urban areas, it has become a rarity and an economic privilege to have easy access to parks, gardens, greenery, or open spaces in which to walk barefoot in the grass or absorb the healing rays of the sun. Studies show not only that there is a strong correlation between people's experience of beauty in their environment and their sense of life satisfaction but also that there are similarities in what environments people prefer. The consensus in many urban areas is that a great deal of current architecture is disliked, especially that which has its design origin in the modernist style.

Modernism, also called international style or international modernism, was dominant in the West from the 1930s to the 1960s. Following the rule that "form follows function," architects of that time focused on what a building should achieve in terms of functionality rather than what it looked like and favored the use of industrial materials such as glass, steel, and concrete. While one could undoubtedly find some local or international examples of modernist buildings that many people might evaluate as aesthetically successful, there are, unfortunately, countless buildings based on that style that would not achieve that standard.

It is interesting to note that while modernist-influenced buildings often meet the second and third of Denis Dutton's three criteria of beauty mentioned in the previous chapter (that is, they may be fit for purpose and be well-executed), they do not meet the first criterion because they do not present shapes or features, such as curves or nature symbols, that we find inherently pleasurable. As a result, they are experienced as dehumanizing and oppressive rather than spiritually uplifting.

Modernism, Trauma, and Mental Disorders

Many historians of architecture have proposed that a major reason for the rise of modernism in the early twentieth century is that its stark designs reflected the physical, moral, and spiritual wreckage resulting from World War I.

continued

Recently, other researchers, including those in the mental health field, have suggested that while that explanation has merit, we might also consider that the key founders of that style may have experienced either physical brain alterations due to the trauma of World War I, such as PTSD (Post-Traumatic Stress Disorder) or, like Le Corbusier, the Swiss-French architect who is considered the father of modernism, had genetic brain disorders such as ASD (Autism Spectrum Disorder). If that is the case, brain abnormalities could have interfered with their ability to process visual stimuli normally, which led to them limiting visual stimulation in their designs. Mental disorders also might have compromised their ability to understand and empathize with others' emotions and needs.

If this proposition is true, it helps clarify why the influential figures who promoted modernism were not inspired to create buildings that the average person would find attractive. Researchers Ann Sussman and Katie Chen proposed that the detachment people often feel in urban settings and around modern buildings *closely mirrors the disconnect people with PTSD and ASD often have towards others. It all makes a great deal of sense once you think about it: people who are relationally compromised can't come up with an architecture that promotes relationships."*[3]

Even as ugly buildings continue to blight our urban and rural landscapes, there are community initiatives underway worldwide with the common goal of persuading architects, city planners, and property developers to return to more classically informed and human-oriented designs and construct buildings that would last for generations.

"Architectural Uprising," founded in Sweden in 2014, is

one social media movement that objects to the "continued uglification" of developments in Nordic cities. According to Norwegian architect Kurt Singstad: ". . . we have to build in a way that makes the building loved by the public, by its users. . . . I think it is more important than ever that buildings are considered beautiful by those who are not architects or experts on aesthetics."[4] On an ironic note, surveys of architects consistently reveal that most of those who design modern buildings, especially modernist-inspired towers or avant-garde structures, themselves prefer to live and work in buildings with traditional styling.

ART

A related aspect of our culture that has degenerated into much ugliness is art. This is especially the case regarding works that are heavily promoted and featured in the world's major galleries, museums, and private collections, as well as those meant for prominent outdoor public display. Those latter works, like modernist architecture, have unfortunately contributed to the visual deterioration of many of our cities.

Artist and art historian Jane Evershed has done extensive research into how modern and contemporary art has been compromised and manipulated by powerful social, political, and commercial forces. Indeed, she sees the evolution of art within these movements as being a visual metaphor for everything problematic that has been transpiring in our world. ("Modern art" technically refers to work produced from the

1860s to the 1970s and "contemporary art" to work produced from the 1980s to the present day, but sometimes the descriptor "modern" is used to refer to both art movements.)

Evershed's thesis is that art has become one of the most controlled areas of society because it provides easy access through our eyes—our windows of the soul—into the human psyche. The result is that art-making, an activity that once served to edify and uplift the human spirit, has now been appropriated to serve a sociopolitical agenda that is designed to debase human beauty and consciousness through the promulgation of images of violence, physical distortion, and sexual degradation. When beauty and consciousness are debased, people are much more susceptible to the directives and demands of external authorities.[5]

Many famous artworks from the past and present century support Evershed's argument that the inclusion in art of violent, dehumanizing, or degrading imagery (including pornographic imagery) has escalated rapidly over time. Relevant examples from the early years of the modern art movement are Pablo Picasso's *Les Demoiselles d'Avignon* (1907), a painting that features fractured and angular human figures; Marcel Duchamp's *Fountain* (1917), a repurposed urinal; and Man Ray's *Object to Be Destroyed* (1932), an altered metronome conceived as a visual attack on a former lover. Such images were controversial when they first appeared and might still puzzle or unsettle some viewers today.

But the emotional and psychic impact of these past works pales in comparison to that of the more intense images found in many contemporary works—works that might evoke shock and disgust from even the most tolerant and jaded audience members. Some (relatively mild) examples are Chris Ofili's portrait *The Holy Virgin Mary* (1996), made with elephant dung, and Ai Weiwei's deliberate smashing of a million-dollar Han Dynasty vase (1995). A more recent example is the work of Patricia Piccinini, who creates surreal drawings and hyperrealistic and grotesque sculptures of hybrid animals and vehicular creatures. Her stated intentions are that these pieces are meant to examine the increasingly amorphous boundaries between the artificial and the natural in contemporary culture; question how technology affects our understanding of what it means to be human; and urge the viewer to see beauty in all forms of existence. These intentions are commendable and thought-provoking but perhaps too cerebral for many viewers to relate to with positivity when confronted by her highly discomforting images.

The prevailing iconoclastic ideology of modern art also dominates the curriculum of most art schools and prevents aspiring artists from expressing alternative personal visions—as is the case with modern design in architecture schools. When recalling her experience in art school, one former student said: "Modern art is the death of creativity for me. I felt like I died inside when I was doing art to conform in order to get my degree . . . They wanted me to do more messes than create art I would be proud of."[6]

The vital importance of beauty and art to humanity's positive conscious evolution is precisely why it can be so effectively utilized for social engineering purposes. While that truth speaks to the power of established art movements to continue to shape our values and experiences to the negative, it also holds out potential for art's—and our own—positive transformation. Both artists and the public can choose to advocate for and reclaim beauty in the art world by withdrawing their energy, attention, and financial support from any institutions, organizations, or creative endeavors that, in their view, do not affirm life and then purposefully direct their resources toward those that do.

SOUND

Another key issue in regard to ugliness in our environments is the experience of sound. It is critical for our physical and mental health to be able to mitigate the sounds around us. Nowadays, most urban and many rural dwellers are inundated with invasive, unpleasant, and unnatural sounds such as traffic, horns, sirens, construction, and loud music, all of which can have negative health effects. Not only do high levels of environmental noise have the potential to damage the auditory system, but chronic low-level noise is also known to cause mental distress resulting in sleep disturbances, increased stress hormones, and cardiovascular complications.

Chronic low-level noise in our living spaces often comes from sources we have the power to adjust or eliminate, such as the sound of a television, radio, or computer, but it may also come from external sources that we have little or no control over. Unfortunately, restful, restorative silence or environments free of unwanted manmade sounds have become increasingly rare. In response, many individuals and groups have taken action in recent years in the form of public awareness campaigns and petitions to offending individuals, industries, and regulatory bodies to try and reduce the barrage of noise around us, particularly in urban settings. One anti-noise initiative that has garnered support in many cities is the restriction or outright banning of leaf blowers, especially those that are gas-powered, due to their high sound level as well as the amount of dangerous pollutants they emit.

On a more personal level, even much of the music we invite into our lives may be stressful to our systems, whether we are aware of it or not. In 1955 the standard tuning pitch of music was changed—reportedly due to an initiative proposed by the Rockefeller Foundation—from 432 hertz (Hz) to 440 Hz and adopted by the International Organization for Standardization. "Hertz" are vibrational cycles per second, and "standard pitch" is the pitch that, prior to 1955, had been used for the tuning of musical instruments in the Western world and the frequency at which recorded music has been mastered for the past several decades. According to music historian Mark Devlin:

> This decision perplexed musicologists, who maintained that 440 (described as "equal temperament" or "concert tuning,") was anything but the sensible choice that 432 (known as "just intonation,") was. 432 is said to synchronise with the rhythms of human brainwaves,

the rest of nature, and with the frequency of the earth itself, and music performed to that pitch is thought to therefore have healing, or at the very least, soothing and calming properties. . . . 440, in contrast, was thought disturbing and dissonant on an unseen level, with music performed at that pitch having unsettling effects on those exposed to it.[7]

The musician Maria Renold carried out extensive research over twenty years, comparing the effect on audiences of tuning instruments at either 440 Hz or 432 Hz. She concluded that 90 percent of study participants consistently preferred the lower pitch. The higher pitch was found to be more "irritating, unpleasant, aggressive, making one stressful and nervous," whereas the lower one sounded "right, complete, pleasant, radiant, peaceful, harmonious, heartfelt but leaving one free."[8] Author and health advocate Len Horowitz, among others, also pointed out that 440 Hz vibrates in dissonance with (suppresses) the "love frequency" of 528 Hz, which is said to vibrate with the heart.[9] On a practical level, this means that if you want to relieve stress or just listen to something you find beautiful, you may wish to choose music that is set at 432 Hz or 528 Hz and above.

LANGUAGE

Yet one more example of the slow creep of ugliness into our world is the language that is now used in many private and public contexts. I can only speak knowledgeably about colloquial

North American English, but as one who loves words, I cannot help but notice a dramatic change in recent years as to how many people converse on an everyday basis.

Not only has disrespectful and abusive language become commonplace, the breadth and variation of our shared vocabulary seems severely diminished. See the comments section of most even mildly controversial blog posts or videos for evidence. If we want to live in a kinder and better-functioning society, we need to learn how to respectfully disagree with one another. Also, I encourage those who want to keep their vibrational frequency high to recognize that words are powerful and to pay attention to the ones they use and the ones that are used by others to influence our thoughts, emotions, and behaviors. Words can be used to program us, positively or negatively, especially through repetition, and it can be enlightening (though often disappointing) to learn about the origins of many common words and phrases and their true meanings.

Of course, words can be a lot of fun to play around with, too, especially ones that are beautiful to read or hear or are particularly evocative. Lately I am enjoying "adlubescence" (pleasure or delight), "tirliry-pufkin" (a flirt), "dimpsy" (twilight), "apricity" (the warmth of the sun in winter), and "petrichor" (a distinctive, earthy, usually pleasant odor associated with rainfall that follows a warm, dry period and that arises from a combination of volatile organic oils released from the soil into the air).

Choice of words, along with tone of voice and body language, are also important determinants to the building of harmonious relationships—or conversely to the damaging of them—and to success in the gentle art of seduction where one might call upon assistance from Peitho, the Goddess of Charming Speech and Persuasion, one of Aphrodite's close companions.

VANITY

I have focused thus far on ugliness as it appears in the outer world, but the opposition or negation of beauty also presents itself through the phenomenon of personal vanity. Turning again to the dictionary, *Merriam-Webster* offers two main definitions of "vanity": first, "inflated pride in oneself or one's appearance," and second, "something that is vain, empty, or valueless."[10] It is noteworthy how the second use of the word reinforces the ultimate worthlessness of the attitude described in the first. Vanity is not beauty.

Earlier, I discussed the problems associated with a psychological overidentification with Aphrodite. Vanity—the shadow side of beauty's light—is a common manifestation of such overidentification. And whether experienced or displayed by an individual or a group, vanity is a serious impediment to personal and spiritual growth. It is a cliché to say that "true beauty lies within," but just because that sentiment is familiar does not mean that it has been genuinely adopted by society at large.

Collectively, we still very much value the outward physical appearance of ourselves and others. Some of that attachment is normal and understandable; scientific research has consistently found that perceptions of human beauty, based on fundamental facial structure as determined by the golden ratio, appear to be universal across cultures and remain essentially unchanged over time. So, the fact that we make evaluations about what faces, bodies, or physical adornments—including our own—we think are beautiful is inevitable and need not be a cause for concern. The psychological problem of vanity (or its opposite, extreme self-criticism) arises only when our ego-attachment to appearance becomes inflated, and we lose sight of the importance of other aspects of the self, particularly the heart and soul. Astrologer Andrew Smith addressed this dark side of the energy of Venus, the Morning Star:

> The world of matter is beautiful, enchanted by spirit and enlivened by the soul, a world brought alive by those who "hear" and "see" the essence that lies within. . . . [But] as the world is encouraged away from its spiritual origins, matter and form has become deified. . . . When the quest for self-worth becomes entangled with the external gaze of others, the purity of your spiritual essence is overshadowed. . . . You are not merely your body, your figure, your skin, your face, your form. Your beauty lies within. What you create with your presence, is beauty. What comes from your heart, is what allures, entices and attracts. Not the pose, the pout or the suggestion. Before you ask someone to look in your mirror, have [you] paused to reflect on why their gaze and attention is important?

Do you "see" you? Do you "like" you? Do you know the beauty that resides inside you?[11]

[I] came to view that in writing about beauty as a philosopher, I was addressing the deepest kind of issue there is. Beauty is but one of an immense range of aesthetic qualities ... But beauty is the only one of the aesthetic qualities that is also a virtue, like truth and goodness. It is not simply among the values we live by, but one of the values that defines what a fully human life means.

—ARTHUR C. DANTO, *The Abuse of Beauty*

WHAT GETS IN THE WAY OF EXPERIENCING BEAUTY?

I mentioned in the previous chapter how we often separate ourselves from directly experiencing beauty through electronic mediation. Similarly, we can distance ourselves from beauty due to inner blocks. (This is also true for other pleasurable experiences such as love and positive physical sensations.) Beauty can manifest in a myriad of ways and can be found almost anywhere, if only in trace amounts and if we are committed to discovering it. The possibility of experiencing beauty in some form is almost always present.

Despite this, in my work as a psychologist, I regularly see people who struggle to recognize and appreciate beauty in their own lives and in the world around them. Adverse life experiences such as abuse, neglect, violence, loss of loved ones, poverty, and negative programming from parents and society at large all leave deep wounds that can impair a person's ability to access beauty. These are not just individual occurrences; we have collectively rejected the values of Aphrodite and the Divine Feminine in many aspects of life and so have cut ourselves off from the experience of beauty's transformative power.

Henry David Thoreau famously wrote, "The mass of men lead lives of quiet desperation."[12] From my clinical experience, I would expand his statement to read, "The mass of people lead lives of fear and chronic stress leading to never-ending struggle and quiet desperation." There is often little time or space given in the midst of that struggle and desperation to experience what could be truly nourishing to the soul.

Unfortunately, the formal study and practice of psychology, as we have come to know it, has done little to ameliorate our disconnection from beauty. Most modern approaches to psychology do not reflect the original meaning of the term—which was the study of the soul—and are now associated more strictly with the study of the mind and behavior. These are important areas of concern, to be sure, but there is little corresponding focus or even inclusion by researchers and practitioners in the field on the importance of beauty to our mental and physical health. Jungian psychologist James Hillman repeatedly took psychology to task for repressing the vital role that beauty plays in our well-being:

> [The] curious refusal to admit beauty in psychological discourse occurs even though each of us knows that nothing so affects the soul, so transports it, as moments of beauty—in nature, a face, a song, an action or dream. And we feel that these moments are therapeutic in the truest sense: make us aware of soul and make us care for its value. We have been touched by beauty. Yet . . . therapy never discusses this fact in its rhetoric, and the aesthetic plays no role whatsoever in therapeutic practice, in developmental theory, in transference, in the notions of successful treatment or failed treatment, and the termination of therapy. Are we afraid of its power?[13]

Even though so much of psychology (as well as other fields of endeavor devoted to mental and physical health) has generally failed us in acknowledging the power of beauty, we can always choose as individuals to turn our gaze away from what is ugly—or that which makes the soul "shrink within itself" as Plotinus phrased it—and look toward the beautiful. By so doing we can fashion different and better lives. Also, nature, if not interfered with, continues to offer us an incalculable number of beautiful experiences that can function as antidotes to our experiences of ugliness in the world.

I frequently ask clients a question at the end of a first

session: "If you could have your life however you want it to be, what would it look like?" or alternatively, "What would it mean to you to live a beautiful life?" Occasionally, someone will describe a hedonistic scenario in which they have buckets of money, a life of leisure, a big house, and a fancy car. More commonly, clients' imagined scenarios are modest: "I would have a job I liked," "I would not have to work so much, and I could see my kids more," "I would be able to buy a small apartment," "I would not feel sick all the time." Sometimes, a person who is depressed will say they cannot imagine a positive future at all. There is no wrong answer to this question, and any response tells me a great deal about a person's values, aspirations, and state of mind, information that we can then explore together.

What has struck me over the years, though, is how *very* modest so many of my clients' scenarios are given that my invitation in the exercise is to imagine a life *however you want it to be*. I am not insensitive to the very real financial, health, familial, or other restrictions that may be in place for any individual when they give their answer or to the fact that some people may prefer to live very simple lives or are generally content with their lives as they are.

At the same time, I want to point out the psychological limitations that are in place for many people who have not recognized their own power to choose or given themselves permission to change aspects of their lives that are unsatisfying, unhealthy, or in some way self-limiting or self-destructive, or even to contemplate what it would mean to have a truly meaningful, nourishing, and beautiful life. Thankfully, there is an antidote to this limiting perspective, and it can be found in our attention to and conscious embodiment of Aphrodite's gift of beauty.

Chapter 8

Love, Beauty, and the Senses

Though the joy and sadness [of being in the world] will
come and go, the more we let the current of life through
our senses, the more we may feel what it is like to belong.
Belonging in the world, sensing our kinship with it, gives rise to
commitment; ... Commitment is an expression of trust; and we
trust when we sense we are of the same substance of another,
and as the world. Knowing ourselves to be of one body with life,
suffused with it, we can throw ourselves wholeheartedly into the
business of living it, without any reason to hold back.

—ROGER HOUSDEN, *Soul and Sensuality*

As I discussed in Chapter 5, the term "erotic," which comes
from Eros's name, need not have only explicitly sexual
connotations. It can also be used to describe a more lovingly
connected, pleasurable, and soulful response to life, one that
goes beyond an automatic stimulus-response or purely sensa-
tion-based reaction.

A simple but deeply rewarding way each of us can develop and sustain more eroticism in our lives is to engage with our bodily senses mindfully and with discernment. If we take to heart the value of giving careful sensuous attention to whomever or whatever we love—be it a romantic or sexual partner, friend, pet, garden, physical space, treasured object, or even an activity—we can bring more beauty and enjoyment to that area of our lives. Such attention need not only be directed outward. We can express love for ourselves in the same way.

ATTEND TO YOUR SENSES

Most everyone would be able to identify five distinct bodily senses that we use to decipher and understand the world: smell, taste, hearing, sight, and touch. Many researchers, however, believe we have at least seven bodily senses. The two commonly added to the list are vestibular (the perception of our body in relation to gravity, movement, and balance) and proprioception (knowing where our body parts are and how we are positioned in space). Others say we likely have many more senses than that, plus numerous potentially powerful non-physical sensory capabilities, such as intuition, that are often undeveloped or downplayed. Our senses are also not completely distinct ways of perceiving; they can be interconnected physiologically and psychologically. Still, we are most familiar with the basic five, so it is those I highlight here.

When we consider beauty, we tend to think of perceiving

it visually and aurally, but all our senses can be involved in the process of evaluating whether something is beautiful to us or not. Of course, other people may disagree about what constitutes beauty in any particular instance, and such disagreements are often based on previous sense-associative experiences. For instance, research on odor-associative learning has found that how you *feel* when you first encounter a particular scent will determine your future hedonic perception of it. That is, we like odors we first encountered when we were happy or odors that are connected to something that has positive meaning for us, and we dislike odors we first encountered when we were unhappy in some way or those connected to something that has negative meaning for us.[1] An example of odor association from my own life is my reaction to the smell of sawdust. It triggers fond memories of my father, who had a workshop that always smelled of sawdust in the basement of our family home.

Although the same type and amount of research has not been conducted with every sense I discuss in this chapter, we can reasonably extrapolate these odor-associative findings to our other senses, at least to some degree. As you read the following, consider what associations—positive or negative—you have to various sensory stimuli. You can use this information to intentionally engage each of your senses and then allow that sense to guide you toward an experience of pleasure and a heightened awareness of the beauty around you—a true Aphrodisian pursuit.

BREATHE IN BEAUTY

Our sense of smell (or olfaction) is our most primitive sense, and it is one of our most sensitive. Researchers estimate that humans can distinguish more than one trillion scents. Smell is also one of the most difficult senses to turn off, likely because it is so vital to our survival. Our sense of smell can alert us to dangers such as bad food or the presence of dangerous animals, gasses, or chemicals in our environment. Smell can also help us navigate geographically, find food and water, communicate with others, and even find a desirable mate.

According to author Rachel Herz, "Our sense of smell is essential to our humanity, emotionally, physically, sexually, and socially. Without a sense of smell, our ability to know ourselves and others is obscured, our emotional world becomes deadened or disturbed, our ability to enjoy food is lost; our health may decline; and sexual desire, and even our capability to identify with whom it would be biologically best to conceive a child, is severely weakened."[2]

The internet is replete with lists of smells that are said to induce various aspects of well-being. Such lists are particularly popular with commercial scent providers and real estate / home staging consultants who strive to shape our moods through the targeted use of smell. But we also have very personal associations with smells. Our olfactory glands are closely linked to the parts of our brain that process emotions and memory.

We have probably all had the experience of having an intense feeling or memory triggered by a particular smell. This is often referred to as the "Proust effect" in reference to the famous passage from Marcel Proust's novel *Swann's Way* in which the scent and taste of linden tea and a madeleine cookie mentally transports the protagonist to an earlier time in his life. Proust later termed this phenomenon "involuntary memory": "No sooner had the warm liquid mixed with the crumbs touched my palate than a shiver ran through me and I stopped, intent upon the extraordinary thing that was happening to me. An exquisite pleasure had invaded my senses, something isolated, detached, with no suggestion of its origin."[3]

Proust's contemporary, Rudyard Kipling, is also known for memorializing this phenomenon in his poem "Lichtenberg" about an Australian soldier in South Africa who smells the blossoms of a golden wattle tree and longs for his homeland:

Smells are surer than sounds or sights
To make your heart-strings crack—
They start those awful voices o'nights
That whisper, "Old Man, come back!"[4]

While Proust's Swann and Kipling's soldier demonstrate a keen awareness of the smells they encounter, we can be affected by odors even if we are not conscious of their presence or cannot identify them. For example, humans silently broadcast our sexual attraction and availability to one another through the release of pheromones, bodily chemicals we excrete that signal sexual arousal, hormone levels, and fertility. We can also be unconsciously affected biologically and emotionally by aromatics in the environment, such as synthetic perfumes or natural scents, including herbs, spices, trees, or flowers.

The writer Diane Ackerman attributed the excitatory power of floral scents to flowers' robust and energetic sex life: "A flower's fragrance declares to all the world that it is fertile, available, and desirable, its sex organs oozing with nectar. Its smell reminds us in vestigial ways of fertility, vigor, life-force, all the optimism, expectancy, and passionate bloom of youth. We inhale its ardent aroma and, no matter what our ages, we feel young and nubile in a world aflame with desire."[5]

Roses are one of my favorite flowers, and I always try to have some in my home for their scent as well as their visual beauty. Unfortunately, many commercial roses have little fragrance. It is always a delight to find those that do, as well as to secure any fresh, sweet-smelling blooms from a garden. I also like knowing roses are considered Aphrodite's signature flower because of their sensual nature. Crispin Sartwell extolled the beauty of roses in his essay on *yapha*, the Hebrew word for "glow" or "bloom":

> Whereas the lily is proverbially pure, being an attribute of the Virgin, the rose is surely fundamentally sensual, a quality signaled by its scent and the profusion of its petal structures and the richness of its colors. Indeed, the literature of the rose is a sort of basting in the senses, a concentration and refinement of sensuality to the point of exquisiteness or preciousness . . . And of course, roses are as well famous for their scent, which seems somehow to correspond to their visual forms, so

that the essence of a rose is both symbolic and a demonstration of the possibility of experiencing beauty in scent.[6]

Given how powerfully smells can affect our mood, alertness, stress, and energy levels, it is worth investigating how you can consciously introduce beneficial aromas into your life. Suggestions for the hedonic and therapeutic use of perfumes, essential oils, herbs, candles, room sprays, and the like are easily found in books and online. This is also the specialty area of aromatherapists who recommend or create blends of plant oils for their clients for aesthetic, relaxation, and healing purposes. Furthermore, health practitioners from many disciplines routinely advise that breathing deeply is good for us physically and mentally. I will add that it is vital for us emotionally and spiritually, too, if what we are breathing in deeply is beauty.

There is perhaps no greater written tribute to the sensuality of scent than the Bible's *Song of Solomon*. This excerpt is from Part 4, "Solomon Admires His Bride":

"The Bridegroom"
You have captured my heart,
my sister, my bride;
you have stolen my heart with one glance of your eyes,
with one jewel of your neck.
How delightful is your love,
my sister, my bride!

Your love is much better than wine,
and the fragrance of your perfume than all spices.
Your lips, my bride,
drip sweetness like the honeycomb;
honey and milk are under your tongue,
and the fragrance of your garments
is like the aroma of Lebanon.
My sister, my bride, you are a garden locked up,
a spring enclosed, a fountain sealed.
Your branches are an orchard of pomegranates
with the choicest of fruits, with henna and nard,
with nard and saffron, with calamus and cinnamon,
with every kind of frankincense tree,
with myrrh and aloes,
with all the finest spices.
You are a garden spring,
a well of fresh water
flowing down from Lebanon.[7]

TASTE BEAUTY

Food is the most obvious substance that we taste, and as with all our senses, our evaluations of what foods taste good to us are personal though they are often strongly rooted in culture. Our sense of taste is also closely intertwined with our sense of smell. Scientists say our sense of taste on its own is highly limited; we can taste only sweet, salty, sour, bitter, and umami. The first four of these were long considered the only basic tastes, but as of 2006, umami—often described as meaty, broth-like, or savory—was added to the list.

Much of what we consider a food's taste or flavor (a more encompassing term) is actually dependent on its aroma. The basic taste of a food plus its aroma—at an estimated ratio of 20 percent taste to 80 percent aroma—is what comprises our main experience of a food's flavor, but the texture, temperature, color, and intensity or "painfulness" (spiciness) of a food can also affect our taste and overall flavor perceptions.

As Proust described, just as smell can evoke powerful memories, so can taste:

> . . . when from a long-distant past nothing subsists, after the people are dead, after the things are broken and scattered, taste and smell alone, more fragile, but more enduring, more immaterial, more persistent, more faithful, remain poised a long time, like souls, remembering, waiting, hoping, amid the ruins of all the rest; and bear unflinchingly, in the tiny and almost impalpable drop of their essence, the vast structure of recollection. Remind us, waiting and hoping for their moment, amid the ruins of everything else; and bear unfaltering in the tiny and almost impalpable drop of their essence, the immense architecture of memory.[8]

Some taste experiences based on pleasurable memories can be relived, and of course, new taste-associative memories can be made. But some may need to be protected by *not* reliving them. To cite a personal example, there is a kind of strawberry-flavored candy I loved as a child and that I still sometimes see for sale. I may very well have classified its taste as beautiful when I was very young—though I probably would not have used that descriptor—but I know I would find it sickly sweet and artificial tasting now, so I am never tempted to buy any. I want to keep my memory of relishing that flavor intact.

Our experience of the taste and enjoyment of food is typically heightened within social contexts. We all know that eating with others and the sharing of food are ancient social and cultural bonding experiences. This is true for gatherings of friends, family, work colleagues, or romantic partners. As the Roman philosopher Epicurus advised, "We should look for someone to eat and drink with before looking for something to eat and drink."[9]

We have also long associated food with expressions of love, and those associations appear even in our words of endearment. Intimate partners and loving parents alike often refer to the objects of their affection by the names of food: pumpkin, peanut, *mon petit chou* (my little cabbage), cookie, or sweetie pie. Sharing food and drink is also an integral element of most courtship and seduction rituals, and there is a rich history of employing food specifically for aphrodisiac purposes—a subject I explore in Chapter 9.

For now, whether you are dining alone or with others, I invite you to attend mindfully to the choice, preparation, and presentation of your food and how, where, and in what context you consume it. I recommend expressing appreciation for your food as you prepare it (and notice how food prepared when you are in a good mood turns out versus when you are in a bad mood) and then blessing your food before you eat it.

The effects of these actions may not be only psychological; many people believe that the actual chemical structure of food and beverages can be beneficially transformed by positive words and thoughts, as Masaru Emoto detailed in his book *The Hidden Messages in Water*.[10] Even if you do not believe this is possible, directing positive energy toward both the preparation and consumption of what you eat and drink could change your emotional state, which would, in turn, affect your response to what is on your plate or in your glass.

Then, slow down so you can notice and savor your food's full flavor. Some people worry that giving too much attention to the experience of eating will lead to overindulgence. Researchers have found that the opposite is usually the case. Chronic deprivation, as opposed to intentional, limited periods of fasting, tends to intensify cravings and increase consumption of restricted or unhealthy foods. Eating what is truly physically nourishing and satiating, as well as what one finds sensuously satisfying, can result in a reduction of the overall amount of food consumed.

Also, by being fully and erotically present to the experience of eating, you can change that ordinary act to one that is meaningful, even sacred, whether you are alone or with someone else. Furthermore, being fully present to the experience of eating can be especially important for those who have a history of disordered eating. Developing awareness of the conscious and unconscious drivers of one's relationship with food is an important component in the process of changing problematic eating patterns.

LISTEN TO BEAUTY

I addressed earlier the importance of being aware of the quality of the sounds around you and attending wherever possible to those that give you pleasure. For some, the most beautiful sounds will always be those from nature and living things—including the sounds of people they care about. Others may prefer to attend to music or other human-made sounds. Music can create strong emotional responses ranging from sadness and despair to hopefulness and ecstasy, and it can help us communicate feelings and intentions without the use of words. This is true cross-culturally, even though the music that produces any particular response may differ widely from one culture to another.

In terms of pleasure, research has shown that listening to music we enjoy can significantly increase dopamine levels in the brain.[11] Also, like smell and taste, music can evoke strong memories, and those associated memories can usually be easily recalled. For instance, it is a common occurrence for couples to designate a song as "theirs," and hearing that song will immediately evoke feelings about their relationship. As long as the romance continues, those feelings are likely to be positive, but if it sours or ends, hearing that same song could quickly prompt feelings of sorrow or anger.

Once again, an Aphrodisian approach would be to bring into your environment sounds that will affect you as you wish to be affected or affect others. Some days, you may wish to listen to rousing music that will fill up the space you are in and get you moving. Other days, you may wish to focus on a small comforting sound like a cat's purr or just stop what you are doing and tune into the variety of sounds that may surround you at that moment. Something I personally value is listening to poetry. The sight of a poem on a page can be beautiful to me depending on the layout and typeface used, but the experience of that poem can become even more meaningful if I hear the words spoken—by someone who has a voice I find pleasing, of course!

You can also take the initiative to create sounds that give you pleasure—either through playing an instrument, singing, or chanting. (These activities have also been linked to better brain health throughout the life span.) I used to belong to an improvisational singing group, and not only was it great fun to play around with different musical notes and rhythms, it helped me stay sensitive to the beauty of the sounds that I and the other group members could spontaneously create. Not every improv session was as satisfying as another. Sometimes our collaborations did not work out musically and devolved into a lot of silliness and laughter, but at other times, our voices came together to create music that was deeply satisfying and that transported us to a different experiential realm.

Research evidence shows that some music and sound frequencies can be emotionally and physically healing, and practitioners from many cultures offer sound healing using various musical instruments, including gongs or crystal bowls. Acoustics scientist John Stuart Reid affirmed that many health challenges can be alleviated by exposure to certain frequencies and reported that his own chronic back pain was eliminated by immersion in low-frequency sound.[12]

Similarly, music professor Giovanna Conti, when dealing with her own health problems, discovered that the structure of some classical music (such as works by Beethoven, Chopin, and Mozart) accords with the healing principles of GNM (German New Medicine), an approach that explores the connection between patients' psyches and their diseases.

Ryke Hamer, the founder of GNM, conducted extensive research into this phenomenon and concluded that certain pieces of music (ideally listened to at 432 Hz) can have a positive impact on the nervous system.[13] Other researchers have been exploring specifically how hearing music that was meaningful in the past can have a healing effect on people with neurodegenerative diseases.

A moving example of this effect is shown in a video posted in 2020 by the Asociación Música para Despertar (Music Association for Awakening), a Spanish charity that uses music to improve the lives of dementia patients. In that video, Alzheimer's patient Martina Gonzalez, a former ballerina, is emotionally and physically transformed as she listens to a recording of Tchaikovsky's *Swan Lake*. Some critics have questioned the information presented about Gonzalez's past as a dancer, but those concerns do not detract from the therapeutic implications of her expressive and touching "performance."[14]

The absence of sound can also be deeply nourishing, yet too

much silence can leave one feeling disconnected from life. This can be especially acute if the silence is imposed from without or in the case of deafness. Helen Keller famously wrote about the deeper and more complex problems of deafness compared to blindness because it means the loss of the human voice, though this is a view now roundly rejected by many in the deaf community. In any case, we may never be able to experience full silence because our bodies themselves are alive with sounds.

Diane Ackerman referred to these as the "rustling, throbbing, whooshing of our bodies, as well as [their] incidental buzzings, ringings, and squeakings."[15] We may not find pleasure in all our bodily sounds (and some may even be cause for concern), but perhaps we can learn to appreciate them as an indication that we are beautifully alive and our miraculous bodies are continuing to function as they are meant to, even if that means alerting us to problems.

OPEN YOUR EYES TO BEAUTY

Although we may perceive beauty through any of our senses, we are most used to identifying it through our vision, an orientation reflected in the formal study of aesthetics, the branch of philosophy concerned with beauty and taste. Like scholars in that field, when we consider the subject of beauty, we usually focus on what we find beautiful (or not) in an artwork or other object, or a face, body, or natural phenomenon; that is, in something external to us that we can observe. Perhaps we do not need to be taught to see beauty per se (after all, most people have at least some opinions about what they find beautiful) but to expand our vision to see more beauty and then consciously bring it into our lives wherever and whenever we can.

As a child, I liked playing the game "I Spy." It usually went like this: One player would say, "I spy with my little eye something that is . . . " and name a shape or color. Then the other player would need to look around and try to find something that fit that description. If they succeeded, it became their turn to choose, and the game continued until one or both players got tired of it. It is a simple game, but it reflects an important principle: We find what we attend to or, as I often say to my clients (and remind myself), "Energy flows where attention goes." When it comes to finding beauty, it is almost always there somewhere if we search for it, are willing to look in some unexpected places, and allow ourselves to be surprised. Our experience of beauty and of life in general will then follow our perceptions and attention.

Take the beauty of color as an example. A common element of the "I Spy" game was looking for different colors in the environment. It is fun and satisfying to do, even as an adult. A few days prior to writing this section, I went on a search for colorful leaves for an autumnal table centerpiece. Maple trees are plentiful near where I live, but it was late in the season, and from a distance, it appeared that the carpet of fallen leaves around the trees had already faded to a monochromatic dull tan. When I arrived, I stood disappointed for a moment, then spotted the corner of a small red specimen nestled among the older dried and curled ones. I focused my gaze, determined to find another, and the more I explored, the more richly colored leaves I found: red, orange, yellow, and burgundy-toned ones, even a few that were still tinged with green around the edges. They had been there all along; I just had not seen them until I really paid attention. I left with a small but satisfying bundle. (Later, I dried them, and they became a lovely example of *wabi-sabi*.)

I love color—looking at it, wearing it, and having it in my living space. I get hungry for certain colors and go through periods where I just cannot get enough of one or another. I know people whose preference will always be for pale or muted tones. I can appreciate those choices, especially in the context of white linen clothing on a hot summer day or the design of elegant interiors, but I will usually opt for having some degree of color on or around me. This is not only because I find so many colors aesthetically pleasing but also because I am attuned to how color can shape my mood.

It is widely accepted that color has the power to affect us physically and emotionally. For instance, research has demonstrated that warm colors, such as red and orange, increase our physiological and psychological arousal levels, while cool colors, such as blue and green, calm them. This knowledge has been applied to everything from the color choice of stoplights to the decoration of spa retreats. As is the case with aromas, however, how an individual responds to a certain color (or any visual stimulus) can be based on a number of factors, including past associations, familial and cultural history, and current fashion trends.

Only those who love color are admitted to its beauty
and immanent presence. It affords utility to all, but
unveils its deeper mysteries only to its devotees.

—JOHANNES ITTEN, *Kunst der Farbe*

I have a friend, Kora Sevier, who is an architectural color
consultant. Her sobriquet is "The Beautifier," and she has helped
me and many other people over the years enhance the beauty
of our homes and businesses through the skillful introduction
of color. Here are a few of her reflections on her consultation
process with clients:

> During a color consultation I take various color samples
> and place them on a board for the client to see. Often,
> though not always, there is a very interesting thing that
> happens, but it only happens when we are looking at
> samples that have color to them versus, let's say, gray.
> The client will walk over to the board and touch the
> color . . . I am continually struck by this action and
> find it revealing. This desire to touch color speaks to
> our deep love of it . . . the challenge for many people is
> that when they use a color what they are saying is: this
> is who I am, this is my unique self. It leaves one open
> to criticism, but if we can face it our lives will be deeply
> enriched . . . I have seen [color] change people's feelings
> about themselves and about their environment. I have
> seen nothing less than watching them fall in love.[16]

Variations on this same process can be used to enhance your own well-being through attention to beauty—both noticing it in the world and choosing it consciously—in order to bring it into your personal environment. Simply put, this can be done by directing your attention to what you find pleasing and then selecting carefully what you want to keep, discard, or change to create a personal space that feels beautiful and life-enhancing to you.

You can apply the same attention to how you dress. Along with the myriad of images through the ages that have celebrated the beauty of Aphrodite's naked body, there are many that show her in softly draped gowns and adorned with headdresses and precious jewelry. (Given the times we live in and the climate you inhabit, you will probably not want to emulate the former depictions—at least not in public.) Aphrodite is connected to nature, so we might surmise that an Aphrodisian approach to clothes and adornment favors that which is associated with the earth (natural fabrics, colors, stones, metals, for example). But as with your home environment, you do not have to wear clothes that look overtly "earthy" or "spiritual" to evoke the presence of Aphrodite or any other goddess or god. If you like flowing diaphanous garments, wear them! But if you favor the look and feel of tweed, that is good too. For some, wearing crystals, stones, and amulets is an affectation to spirituality; for others, it is a genuine appreciation of the energies of those objects.

Forget the dictates of fashion. What matters is that you choose clothes and accessories that help you express what *you* genuinely want to express about yourself and that help you feel how *you* want to feel. I know of women who are restricted in terms of what they must wear in their work-places, but because that professional "look" does not represent who they truly are, they wear beautiful silk or lace lingerie under their business suits or uniforms to keep them in touch with their Aphrodite nature.

TOUCH BEAUTY

I once encountered a woman in a spa change room (decorated in appropriately serene colors, of course) who vehemently complained to me that the new robes the spa provided were "too fluffy." My first thought was that that was a very odd thing to complain about to a stranger, and my second thought was that she and I lived in very different worlds. In my world, a fluffy robe is a pleasure. As is the feel of warm sand under my feet, the soft velvet of my multicolored sofa cushions, the smooth wooden rolling pin that was made by my father and used by my mother, a full body massage when I really need it (or even when I do not), the buoyant water of a flotation tank, the fuzzy peel and silky flesh of a ripe peach, a freshly ironed cotton shirt, the skin and hair of someone I love . . .

Like sight, our experience of touch is almost always oriented outward to someone else or something outside of ourselves. We can touch our own outer body, of course, but we cannot touch very much of our own insides. We are wired to give and receive touch in order to navigate the world. Our skin, the largest organ of the body, contains millions of sensory receptors that respond to pain, temperature, and pressure. The areas that are the most sensitive to light touch and pressure are our palms, soles, lips, eyelids, genitals, and nipples.

Our sense of touch keeps us physically safe and comfortable and is vital for our physical and emotional health and well-being. Neither humans nor other mammals thrive if they are deprived of positive touch. It is necessary for a child's normal physical and brain development and helps strengthen the immune systems of children and adults.

We can be strongly affected by even a seemingly insignificant touch from another person. According to Dacher Kelter, a professor of psychology and the founder of the Greater Good Science Center, "A pat on the back, a caress of the arm—these are everyday, incidental gestures that we usually take for granted . . . [But] they are far more profound than we usually realize: They are our primary language of compassion, and a primary means for spreading compassion."[17]

And, of course, touch is an important element in intentionally loving encounters with others, whether those encounters are sexual in nature or not. (Sex over the internet or via virtual reality will always come up woefully short in this regard.) Unfortunately, Western society is becoming increasingly touch-deprived as people spend more and more time devoted to their phones and computers instead of interacting with each other in person. To make matters worse, events like the pandemic scare of the early 2020s have actively discouraged people from being in close physical contact with one another.

Even if there is not another person available that you wish to touch or have touch you, you can still nourish your sense of touch by seeking out pleasurable and healthful touch experiences in your environment or through self-touch. Interestingly, researchers consider yoga, as well as self-massage or even exercising while in touch with the ground, to be forms of self-touch that can decrease stress hormones.[18] This last finding is consistent with the objectives of "earthing"—or "grounding" as it is also known—the practice of connecting our bodies directly to the energies of the earth. Earthing not only feels good; it can have restorative physical and psychological health benefits.

In terms of touch experiences that are focused on the sensuous, what do you like to touch and have touching you? Do you like the feel of the clothes and jewelry that you wear, the consistency of the cosmetics or body products that you use, the texture of your furniture or the objects you habitually use? Do you enjoy the mouthfeel of certain foods? And do you pay attention to even small and routine experiences of gratifying touch in your life? For example, I rarely listen to audiobooks. I much prefer to curl up with a tangible book in my favorite spot (usually the bed with lots of down pillows behind me) and take in the full experience of the book's scent, look, and physical feel.

If we use mythological language for [the] inherent radiance [of beauty], we would speak of Aphrodite; the golden one, the smiling one, whose smile made

the world pleasurable and lovely. She was more than
an aesthetic joy; she was an epistemological necessity for without her, all the other Gods would remain
hidden, like the abstractions of mathematics and the-
ology, but never palpable realities ... Owing to her, the
divine could be seen and heard, smelled, tasted and
touched. She made manifest the divine mind. And we
respond to her radiant presence in things with words
like divine, marvelous, gorgeous, superb, wonderful,
amazing, heavenly, delightful, out-of-this-world—
words that attest to the divine enhancement of any
ordinary thing, whether the feel of a fabric, the fall of
a woman's hair, the taste of a wine.

—JAMES HILLMAN, *"The Practice of Beauty"*

TWO MULTISENSORY PURSUITS

If you would like to easily create a beautiful experience that
could simultaneously awaken all the senses explored here, a
familiar but still excellent option is the loving preparation and
presentation of a healthy meal, ideally shared and savored with
a favorite companion, in an aesthetically attractive and physically comfortable environment, the air redolent with delicious
aromas, and with soft pleasing music in the background. If you
would like to make this a specifically aphrodisiac meal to be
enjoyed with someone special, you may wish to follow some of
the suggestions offered in the next chapter.

Another quite different but equally beautiful choice for a
multisensory experience could be the healing activity of forest

bathing or *shinrin-yoku*, the Japanese practice of visiting a forest and breathing its air. This ancient nature practice is known to reduce stress, depression, and anxiety and increase immune function. It is interesting to consider that perhaps one reason the experience of forest bathing is so beneficial is because it could involve the activation of four of the main senses—smell, hearing, sight, and even touch—thereby helping a person feel fully connected to and alive in their bodies. The only sense that might not be activated by this activity is taste—unless the forest bather were to bring along their own picnic or decide to sample the forest flora, in which case, one hopes they know what they are doing!

BODY AWARENESS

The energy of Aphrodite and the Divine Feminine is always grounded in the body, and a key component to creating a rich erotic life is learning how to love and accept our bodies and embody our experiences. The two multisensory activities just presented, if undertaken consciously, can certainly increase sensuous awareness, but it would still be possible to participate in them and remain disconnected from the experience of our physicality as a whole. It takes discipline and dedication to stay fully present to our bodily sensations (along with our thoughts and emotions), as anyone who has ever tried mindfulness or other meditative practices can attest.

As valuable as those approaches are, they are often conducted in ways that emphasize attention to mental rather than physical experiences. There can be great benefit in engaging in practices such as movement-based yoga, tai chi, or conscious/ ecstatic dance. Practices like these are designed to raise awareness of one's body, help release self- and culturally imposed limitations to the full joyous expression of one's individuality, and bring harmony to body, mind, and spirit. This is how Gabrielle Roth, founder of the 5Rhythms movement practice, described her experience of the transformational potential of dance: "To surrender to the dance, to enter its beat and trance, to let it fly, free form, to find unity in moving my body, to express my heart and empty my mind—this is ecstasy, the place where the contraries dissolve and something else is ignited, something deeper, something divine."[19]

In this brief statement, Roth perfectly captured the spiritual nature of her relationship to dance, and it serves as a near template for describing the essence of the relationship to Aphrodite that is possible through the awakening of our senses.

Just as Roth worshiped the spirit of dance rather than its form, we can worship the spirit of Aphrodite without attachment to any particular form of her presence. We can choose to engage consciously with the physical world and actively seek out its beauty—a reflection of Aphrodite's beauty—at any time, and then love and celebrate that beauty through our sensitivities to smell, taste, sound, sight, and touch. That choice will not only enhance our enjoyment of the present moment but it can also inspire us to adopt a view of life that is less focused on the intellect and more expansively heartfelt. That, in turn, may lead us to experience "something deeper, something divine" within ourselves, as Roth termed it, as well as an awareness of the force that connects us all.

The experience of the Divine in whatever form it reveals itself can be awe-inspiring, but that does not mean it has to be solemn (just as conscious or ecstatic dance may be serious in its intent but not solemn in its execution). One lighthearted way to celebrate love and beauty through our senses is through the enthusiastic and mindful preparation, consumption, and sharing of sensuous foods and drinks. These culinary acts are, of course, a direct expression of Aphrodisian values as they pertain to the connections between food, sex, and love.

Chapter 9

Aphrodisiacs

Like most other humans, I am hungry ... it seems to me that our
three basic needs, for food and security and love, are so mixed
and mingled and entwined that we cannot straightly think of one
without the others. So it happens that when I write of hunger, I am
really writing about love and the hunger for it, and warmth and the
love of it and the hunger for it ... and then the warmth and richness
and fine reality of hunger satisfied ... and it is all one.

—M. F. K. FISHER, *The Gastronomical Me*

No treatise on Aphrodite would be complete without men-
tion of aphrodisiacs. Although her myths do not reveal
what Aphrodite liked to eat, we can imagine that a goddess with
such an appreciation for the earth's bounty—which she helps
to flourish after all—would be a lover of good food, especially
good food that leads to good sex. The lack of mythological ref-
erences notwithstanding, we know that for thousands of years
in Greece and elsewhere, special substances have been used to

enhance the libido and sexual performance of both women and men. We know these substances as "aphrodisiacs," their name derived, of course, from the Goddess of Love herself.

A BRIEF HISTORY

Historically, most aphrodisiacs have been foods or beverages that would have been consumed in preparation for either a quick seduction or a long night of passionate lovemaking, depending on the situation and the desires of the participants. Other substances that would not commonly be considered foods or beverages but which have similarly been reputed to have sexually stimulating properties have been employed for the same purposes. Examples are fragrant body oils, body rubs, perfumes, and incense, along with some decidedly unappealing items—at least to our contemporary sensibilities—including animal parts (especially genitalia), birds' nests, insects, and other items not usually eaten. In many cases, it has been the rarity, illegality, expense, or even the physical risk of consuming such substances that have added to their mystique and fueled the demand for them.

Although we now tend to associate aphrodisiacs with romance—hence the annual lists of aphrodisiac foods that appear in the media every Valentine's Day—aphrodisiacs have been put to some less benign purposes over time. Historical records suggest that although aphrodisiacs have been used primarily to heighten desire, bestow sexual stamina, and encourage fertility, they have also been used to exert power over unsuspecting or reticent sexual targets. Whether or not it is now or ever was possible to seduce a truly unwilling partner by means of an aphrodisiac alone, to use any sexual aid in a manipulative or even perfunctory manner is antithetical to Aphrodite's intent and, in the case of manipulation, contrary to the principle of free will. To be true to her sensibility, the use of an aphrodisiac should be consensual and its experience sensuous and pleasurable in all ways.

Most cultures consider the sharing of a meal to be an essential element of courtship, and the sensual appreciation and consumption of aphrodisiac foods and drinks can add eroticism and mystery to the seduction process. Countless poets have described the delights of preparing and sharing exquisite foods and drinks with one's beloved. This is an excerpt from John Keats's "Eve of Saint Agnes":

> And still she slept an azure-lidded sleep,
> In blanched linen, smooth, and lavender'd,
> While he forth from the closet brought a heap
> Of candied apple, quince, and plum, and gourd;
> With jellies soother than the creamy curd,
> And lucent syrops, tinct with cinnamon;
> Manna and dates, in argosy transfer'd
> From Fez; and spiced dainties, every one,
> From silken Samarcand to cedar'd Lebanon.
>
> These delicates he heap'd with glowing hand
> On golden dishes and in baskets bright
> Of wreathed silver: sumptuous they stand

In the retired quiet of the night,
Filling the chilly room with perfume light.—
"And now, my love, my seraph fair, awake!
Thou art my heaven, and I thine eremite:
Open thine eyes, for meek St. Agnes' sake,
Or I shall drowse beside thee, so my soul doth ache."[1]

Other writers have sensuously compared their lover's body (or sometimes their own body) with the feel, taste, or scent of enticing foods. A beautiful example is the poem "Srngarakarika" from the twelfth-century Sanskrit epic about the adventures (erotic and otherwise) of a character named Kumaradadatta:

Her breath is like honey spiced with cloves,
Her mouth delicious as a ripened mango.
To press kisses on her skin is to taste the lotus,
The deep cave of her navel hides a store of spices
What pleasure lies beyond, the tongue knows,
But cannot speak of it.[2]

CULINARY CONSIDERATIONS

Despite such sensuous descriptions or the ubiquity of those Valentine's Day lists, when many people think of aphrodisiacs, they conjure up images of weird or exotic ingredients and do not realize that a potential banquet of delicious, nourishing, and effective aphrodisiac foods are all around them and easily obtainable.

To begin cultivating a broader view of aphrodisiac foods,

think of them as being divided into two main categories. The first category is comprised of those items that are said to enhance, through their chemical composition, one's sexual desire, energy, or prowess. In the West, probably the best-known examples are oysters, chocolate, almonds, figs, strawberries, ginseng, and maca. But beyond these, there is a wide range of other foods said to have aphrodisiac properties due to their healthful nutritional content. These include seafood (mussels, salmon, scallops), common fruits (avocados, grapes, peaches, pomegranates), vegetables (asparagus, beans, peppers, tomatoes), spices (cardamom, cinnamon, ginger), nuts (pine nuts, pistachios, walnuts), herbs (basil, juniper, rosemary), and sweets (honey), to name only a few.

The second category of aphrodisiacs is made up of those foods that arouse the erotic imagination because of how they look, taste, smell, or feel. Most aphrodisiacs in this category also contain compounds that contribute to good sexual health, but these compounds may be in lesser amounts than in foods known primarily for their physiologically stimulating properties. When considering aphrodisiacs in this category, think about what each food might remind you of—not surprisingly, the appearance of many of them mimics female or male sex organs—and also about the erotic multisensory experience of eating them. Some examples are asparagus dripping with butter, bananas, ripe soft cheese, mangoes, papayas, quince, and even lettuce (because it grows straight and tall like a phallus and excretes milky liquid when cut).

Many aphrodisiacs belong in both categories. Oysters are probably the most well-known example of a food that can affect both one's physiology and imagination, and they have long been considered to be the quintessential aphrodisiac. Since ancient times, the Greeks have credited oysters, as well as other shellfish, with having aphrodisiac powers due to their association with Aphrodite and her sea birth. Oysters contain zinc, a mineral known to be an anti-inflammatory and anti-oxidant agent that helps with hormone balance and fertility (through increasing testosterone levels), cell growth and repair, immunity, and digestion. In addition, the look, smell, and taste of oysters are suggestive of female sexual organs.

Other foods identified by the ancient Greeks as having aphrodisiac properties include garlic (used in many dishes to stir the senses), legumes (to strengthen the libido and enhance male virility), anise seeds (to increase sexual desire), and olives. Green olives are said to increase men's virility, while black olives are said to stimulate women's passions. In Aphrodite's birthplace of Cyprus, raw olive oil from wild trees is still considered to be particularly sexually potent.

The ancient Greeks and Romans, as well as many other cultures and religions, have also associated pomegranates with sexuality, seeing them as a symbol of spring, fertility, and rebirth (they resemble human ovaries and produce some of the same hormones) and as a food that has powerful healing properties for both women and men. Although pomegranates do sometimes appear in depictions of Aphrodite, they are more often linked with the goddesses Persephone, Demeter, and Hera. Aphrodite herself is more commonly associated with another aphrodisiac fruit—quinces—which are considered sacred to her. Traditionally, newly married couples in Greece would eat quinces at their wedding feast in honor of the Goddess of Love.

It is worth noting the rarity of meat and other fatty or calorically dense foods in both categories of aphrodisiacs. The absence of such foods is because it has been thought that "heavy" foods such as meat and rich sauces take longer to digest than "light" foods such as seafood, vegetables, and fruit—though advocates of meat-based diets dispute this point. The reasoning has been that digestion diverts energy that could be directed to other more enjoyable activities and physical functions. However, historical accounts suggest that many earlier cultures, including earlier European societies, emphasized the consumption of meat, especially to add vigor to male performance. And as anyone who has ever seen the classic ribald movie *Tom Jones* can attest, eating roast chicken with your fingers can be a very sensual experience![3]

In regard to fruits and vegetables, those that have long been considered aphrodisiacs typically grow naturally in the warm climate of the Mediterranean. They, therefore, would have been easily obtainable by the ancient Greeks and other nearby civilizations. This is not the case, of course, in the parts of the world that have colder climates and shorter growing seasons. Although the same aphrodisiac fruits and vegetables that the Greeks identified may now be available through import, it would be advantageous to seek out local and seasonal equivalents to ensure that the food you are eating is as fresh and nutrient-dense as possible.

That said, now as ever, people have different preferences and energy levels, and it may be that for some people, a hearty steak with bearnaise sauce is exactly what turns them on. Others may desire a very different type of feast. Whatever dishes you choose, enjoy! But keep in mind that it is always advisable to eat slowly and moderately in order to build and maintain your libido over the course of an evening. Overeating, especially carbohydrates, can definitely challenge the digestive system and bring on drowsiness. Also, it is important to drink alcohol judiciously. A little alcohol can be a wonderful stimulant to the libido but too much can be a detriment to follow-through. As Shakespeare wisely observed in *Macbeth*, alcohol "provoketh desire, but takes away the performance."[4]

There is a kind of alchemy in the transformation of
base chocolate into this wise fool's gold, a layman's
magic ... As I work, I clear my mind, breathing deeply.
The windows are open, and the through-draft would be
cold if it were not for the heat of the stoves, the copper
pans, the rising vapor from the melting *couverture*. The
mingled scents of chocolate, vanilla, heated copper,
and cinnamon are intoxicating, powerfully suggestive;
the raw and earthy tang of the Americas, the hot and
resinous perfume of the rain forest. This is how I travel
now, as the Aztecs did in their sacred rituals: Mexico,
Venezuela, Columbia. The court of Montezuma. Cortez
and Columbus. The Food of the Gods, bubbling and
frothing in ceremonial goblets. The bitter elixir of life.

—JOANNE HARRIS, *Chocolat*

BUT DO THEY WORK?

While foods of both aphrodisiac types have been used enthusiastically throughout the ages, there is much skepticism among modern scientists as to whether or not the chemicals in such foods actually have the sexually stimulating effects that are credited to them or if they have them in sufficient quantities to create the desired effect.

Typically, culinary aphrodisiacs have, at worst, been dismissed outright by the scientific establishment or, at best, been viewed as a harmless novelty. At the same time, both research and common sense tell us that there is a strong relationship between general physical health and good sexual functioning. In this regard, recent nutritional research has highlighted the beneficial effects of a diet rich in antioxidants and phytochemicals—compounds that are found in abundance in many traditional aphrodisiacs. Research has also found a strong link between diet and hormone health. Such findings have led some medical researchers to theorize that up to 90 percent of sexual dysfunction in both men and women is due to disorders directly related to diet. As the authors of *Great Food, Great Sex* advised, "It's your plate, not your mate."[5]

To whatever degree aphrodisiac foods contribute physiologically to good health and, therefore, to good sex, undoubtedly the greatest amount of their power lies in their effects on the imagination. To prepare an abundant feast (scarcity is never sexy) of delicious foods and complementary beverages and serve them in a sensuous environment with well-paced loving care and the conscious intention to give pleasure will surely compensate for any "scientifically proven" sexually enhancing chemicals that might be missing. In addition, the experience of having an attractive companion make the effort to prepare such a special feast for your senses can be an aphrodisiac in itself.

———

The poetic meaning of all fruit is essentially sexual. "Every fruit has its secret," D. H. Lawrence insists, its provocative mystery that plays upon our compelling desire to open and to know. The sexual overtones are unmistakable, and even when we speak innocently of getting to the "core" of truth, our language makes unconscious reference to forbidden fruit.

—JOHN & JOAN DIGBY, *Food for Thought*

———

"FIGS" (EXCERPT)

Every fruit has its secret.
The fig is a very secretive fruit.
As you see it standing growing, you feel at once it is
    symbolic:
And it seems male.
But when you come to know it better, you agree with the
    Romans, it is female.

The Italians vulgarly say, it stands for the female part; the
    fig-fruit:
The fissure, the yoni,
The wonderful moist conductivity towards the centre.

Involved,
Inturned,
The flowering all inward and womb-fibrilled;
And but one orifice.

The fig, the horse-shoe, the squash-blossom.
Symbols.

There was a flower that flowered inward, womb-ward;

Now there is a fruit like a ripe womb.
It was always a secret.
That's how it should be, the female should always be secret.

   —D. H. LAWRENCE[6]

—————————————

Chapter 10

Awakening to a New Earth

We shall awaken from our dullness and rise vigorously toward
justice. If we fall in love with creation deeper and deeper,
we will respond to its endangerment with passion.

—SAINT HILDEGARD OF BINGEN, *Scivias*

Life since 2020 has been painful for most everyone: psychologically, emotionally, socially, and perhaps economically and physically. And there are still many challenges ahead as the world works to right itself after the exposure of the dark and corrupt forces that have controlled our lives for so very long. At the same time, there is good reason to believe we are moving toward a much better world. The Great Awakening in consciousness I referred to in Chapter 1 has been gathering speed since we entered the astrological Age of Aquarius on December 21, 2020. That was the date of the great conjunction of Jupiter and Saturn at zero degrees of Aquarius. The Age of Aquarius will be 2,160 years long and is said to usher in a

Golden Age of peace, joy, creativity, harmony, freedom, prosperity, and spiritual liberation. What better guide to a Golden Age than the Golden One herself?

Remember that in addition to love and beauty, a great part of what Aphrodite represents archetypally are the energies of rebirth and renewal. We will need these energies in abundance as we go forward to create a New Earth that is in alignment with the wisdom of the Divine Feminine. Aphrodite may be but one manifestation of the Divine Feminine, but she is an especially powerful one. Even as she has been ignored, diminished, and vilified over the ages, Aphrodite has never been forgotten, nor has she lost her value to the collective.

One reason is that she presides over love and beauty—concerns that are central to our lives. Another is that her divine presence can feel deeply personal and intimate to those who honor her. To be blessed with Aphrodite's loving and enlivening presence is profoundly meaningful, not only in itself but also because it can create a bridge to the experience of something greater. The energetic force of the Divine Feminine—or of the Great Mother, as it is often conceptualized—can be hard to comprehend and identify with directly because it can feel too big and all-encompassing to be personal. At the same time, an understanding and embodiment of Divine Feminine energy is exactly what we need to experience if we wish to achieve balance and harmony between our inner feminine and masculine aspects and ultimately realize our own Divine Human nature.

Practices to honor Aphrodite, such as those described in

Chapter 2, may no longer hold relevance for us, but we can still foster, each according to their own style, a meaningful ongoing relationship with the Goddess that maintains and deepens our connection to both the divine and human realms. This does not mean fashioning new versions of ancient rites, though this could be a rewarding pursuit for some. Elaborate ceremonies, formal rituals, and acts of worship are not necessary. Though, for those who are interested in that approach, several individuals and groups have attempted to recreate authentic liturgy and rituals devoted to Aphrodite and published detailed descriptions of them. (For example, see *Cult of Aphrodite* by Laurelei Black.[1]) It is more important for us to honor the sanctity of our own lives by living in accordance with the sensual, life-affirming, resilient, and passionate spirit that Aphrodite represents and that has the power to positively transform our experience of the world.

Author Jalaja Bonheim eloquently expressed how honoring Aphrodite can open us to the recognition of sexual energy and beauty as gateways to inner knowledge and the divine spark of life:

> . . . though Aphrodite is the goddess of love, lovers are not her only worshippers. She is the source of our longing not only for sexual union but above all for sacred union. By her blessing, artists become creators, and through her touch, souls become intoxicated with the sweet wine of mystical love. She is present in the rush of a new friendship or in the transformative encounter

with another person, an animal, or a landscape. Our sigh of pleasure at the scent of a rose, our surge of enthusiasm over a fresh insight, the way our heart leaps with excitement at the sight of wild geese flying across the pale blue evening sky—all these are tributes to the golden goddess.[2]

An essential component of living in alignment with the values and wisdom of Aphrodite and the greater Divine Feminine is to learn to trust our deepest intuition about what truly matters, what truly serves life, and what truly brings us pleasure—sensual and otherwise. Aphrodite is not about the intellectualization of experience, as valuable as a keen intellect may be. The key to Aphrodite-consciousness is to attend to the wisdom of the body, heart, and soul rather than the demands of the ego. We will then be able to make choices that can reconcile different, often conflicting, aspects of ourselves, including the sexual and the spiritual.

Genuine reverence for Aphrodite and our own divinity means leading a life based in love, beauty, and eroticism; awareness of our senses and our body's true needs; and an unwavering connection to the values of the Divine Feminine, including deep respect for the earth and the cycles of nature. The result of attaining such consciousness will be a soulful life rich in love, joy, and abundance in all good things.

Put on the music and dance now. Your unrestricted,
luscious, rich joy serves not only you but the planet.
So move those lower chakras, open your heart, and let
your life force express itself like the most succulent,
juicy fruit, the most redolent and colorful flower, or
the loudest and most raucous song. After that, make a
commitment to getting rid of all the old emotional tox-
ins that have become stuck inside you so you can live
freely and agelessly.

—CHRISTIANE NORTHRUP, *Goddesses Never Age*

Once we have committed to our own healing journey, we
can actively take our experience of love and beauty into the
world in service to others. This is done not by preaching about
the benefits of Aphrodite-consciousness (though you may
be inspired as I am to share your knowledge and enthusiasm
about it) but by living in the light of the Goddess's highest
divine frequency. Each individual's expression of that light will
be unique, but the brighter your light, the more you can help
others. If your light is very strong, you will be able to positively
influence others simply by exposing them to it. This is no small
thing. Our world is going to need a lot of healing light in the
years to come.

A good way to begin awakening and honoring Aphrodite in
your life is to take the time to discern what it is you truly desire.
It is easy to get caught up in pursuing superficial desires that are
the result of addictions and a conditioned consumerist mind-
set. Satisfying such desires may be pleasing in the moment, but

that pleasure is usually short-lived because it does not reflect one's true appetites. As a consequence, you will keep desiring more, and as the saying goes, "You can never get enough of what you don't really want."

As an antidote to the lure of manipulated desires, consider again the idea that there are identifiable levels of conscious-ness and reflect on what experiences elevate your personal consciousness and bring you a sense of genuine fulfillment. As discussed earlier, the archetype of Aphrodite has a dark side which corresponds to the lower levels of human experience, such as jealousy, anger, and revenge, and too much emphasis on those emotions can pull us *down*. But attention to and embodiment of the higher order of the values she represents regarding love and beauty, along with the practice of grati-tude for what is good in our lives and the positive changes that are afoot, can raise us *up*. And that is what will shape our perceptions and experience of the world going forward, even in the face of great difficulties.

Another perspective on awakening Aphrodite-consciousness comes from a source far from that of ancient Greece: the Navajo people of northeastern Arizona. In Chapter 6, I highlighted the Navajo word *hozho* in the context of beauty and the difficulty of translating *hozho* into English due to its many nuances of meaning. It is a term highly attuned to the intelligence of the Divine Feminine. As well as beauty, the term has been variously associated with goodness, favor, harmony, blessedness, order, and what is ideal in any circumstance. Anthropologist Gladys Reichard defined it as "perfection so far as it is obtainable by man . . . it represents the end toward which not only man, but also supernaturals and time and motion, institutions, and behavior strive."[3]

The opposite of *hozho* is another complex word *hochxq*, which means (approximately) "chaos." *Hochxq* can occur in the world at large or in an individual's life. What is required for rebalancing from *hochxq* is the awareness and ritual application of *hozho*.

As a non-Navajo, I do not pretend to understand the breadth and depth of the meanings of *hozho* and *hochxq*, but I resonate with those terms and they seem appropriate in our current situation as we strive to heal ourselves and our world. Surely, after our long experience of *hochxq*, we are in great need of the balancing force of *hozho* in all senses of that powerful word. Here's a portion of Crispin Sartwell's thoughtful exploration of *hozho*. It suggests to me that we would do well to emulate the Navajo's embodiment of this concept, especially at this time in our history.

> [Hozho] refers above all to the world when it is flourishing; it refers to the community, flourishing in the world; it refers to things we make, which flourish and play a role in the flourishing of other things; and it refers to ourselves, flourishing as makers, as people inhabiting a community that inhabits the world. It is a word for the oneness of all things when they are joined together in a wholesome state. . . . As Gary Witherspoon says in his lovely book *Language and Art in the Navajo Universe*

... "[Hozho] is not an abstractable quality of things or a fragment of experiences; it is the normal pattern of nature and the most desirable form of experience."[4]

We need not attempt to adopt or usurp Navajo cultural traditions in order to take inspiration from those traditions. I propose that we hold the beneficent concept of *hozho* in our minds and hearts at the same time as we honor the presence of Aphrodite and her power to restore love and beauty after even the most devastating losses. (Appropriately, Aphrodite's birth into the world followed a time of chaos and violence amongst the gods.) The task at hand for us all now is, one by one, to shift our lives from any chaos, disorder, disease, and pain in our own lives to experiences of harmony, order, health, and pleasure.

A prime catalyst to the process of making such a positive shift and moving toward personal and community flourishing is to nurture in our lives whatever we experience as loving and beautiful. This can be done through the intentional choice of where we place our attention and energy—mentally and physically—and through the kind and compassionate treatment of ourselves and others. The more we give priority to connecting with love and beauty in the world, the more we will discover that love and beauty are likewise wanting to connect with us.

Wherever snow falls, or water flows, or birds fly,
wherever day and night meet in twilight, wherever
the blue heaven is hung by clouds, or sown with stars,
wherever are forms with transparent boundaries,
wherever are outlets into celestial space, wherever is
danger, and awe, and love, there is Beauty, plenteous
as rain, shed for thee, and though thou shouldest
walk the world over, thou shalt not be able to find a
condition inopportune or ignoble.

—RALPH WALDO EMERSON, *Nature and Other Writings*

We can also choose to actively engage our individual creativity in the service of love, beauty, and the Divine Feminine. Sadly, many people have become only passive consumers of others' creative products. While it is wonderful to appreciate someone else's creative output, it is deeply nourishing for the soul—as well as beneficial for the brain, as neuroaesthetic researchers have pointed out—to engage with one's own imagination and creativity. Indeed, doing so can be a spiritual practice and a sacred and erotic act.

Personally, I enjoy expressing myself through writing, but I also connect to my creativity through interior decorating, carefully choosing my clothes and accessories, singing, dancing, and cooking, among other pursuits. Your creative impulses may lead you in very different directions. What matters is that you give yourself permission to create something that has meaning for you and that produces in you a sense of joy and fulfillment. We likely all have creative abilities and talents that are yet to be realized. To experiment and play in whatever creative realms call to you and then to risk bringing your creativity into the light may engender feelings not only of deep satisfaction and pride in yourself but may also lead to a renewed sense of purpose. Furthermore, the sharing of your creative efforts, if they are produced from love and a desire to engage with beauty, could very well benefit a great many others.

Change is upon us. And if enough of us embrace and allow ourselves to be embraced by the beautiful and loving energy of Aphrodite—and thereby the energy of the greater Divine Feminine—and align with her transformative power, then that change will be positive and long-lasting, and we will be free to live as sovereign beings on a loving, beautiful, and revitalized earth. None of us as individuals can transform the whole world, but we can transform ourselves, and by so doing, little by little, we will transform the world around us.

I leave you with a beautiful translation by Mary Barnard of one of Sappho's most evocative and celebratory poems. It is an inspiring vision of what we can call forth in ourselves and in the collective when we invite in the Goddess:

YOU KNOW THE PLACE: THEN

Leave Crete and come to us
waiting where the grove is
pleasantest, by precincts

sacred to you; incense
smokes on the altar, cold
streams murmur through the

apple branches, a young
rose thicket shades the ground
and quivering leaves pour

down deep sleep; in meadows
where horses have grown sleek
among spring flowers, dill

scents the air. Queen! Cyprian!
Fill our gold cups with love
stirred into clear nectar[5]

Notes

Epigraph

1. Mary Barnard trans., Sappho: A New Translation (University of California Press Books, 2019).

Chapter 1

1. Susie Mackenzie, "The Benign Catastrophist," *The Guardian*, September 6, 2003, https://www.theguardian.com/books/2003/sep/06/fiction.jgballard.

2. Karen Armstrong, *A Short History of Myth* (Canongate, 2005) p. 2.

3. Anatoly Fomenko and Gleb Nosovskiy, "The History of New Chronology," Researches on the New Chronology, April 2001, https://chronologia.org/en/history.html.

4. Mary Barnard trans., *Sappho: A New Translation* (University of California Press Books, 2019) p. 3.

Chapter 2

1. Joseph Campbell, *Goddesses*, ed. Safron Rossi (New World Library, 2013) p. 31.

2. Jamake Highwater, *Myth & Sexuality* (New American Library, 1990) p. 32.

3. Campbell, *Goddesses*.

4. "Aphrodite and the Gods of Love," The J. Paul Getty Museum, 2012, https://www.getty.edu/art/exhibitions/ aphrodite/worship.html.

5. Merlin Stone, *Ancient Mirrors of Womanhood* (Beacon, 1979) p. 379.

6. Charlene Spretnak, *Lost Goddesses of Early Greece* (Beacon, 1992) pp. 71–72.

7. William Blake Tyrrell, trans., *Homeric Hymn to Aphrodite* (University of North Carolina) 2, https://people.uncw.edu/ deagona/LIT/HH%20Aphrodite.pdf.

8. "Aphrodite," *Wikipedia*, https://en.wikipedia.org/wiki/Aphrodite.

9. Agapi Stassinopoulos, *Gods and Goddesses in Love* (Paraview, 2004) p. 30.

10. Clark Strand and Perdita Finn, *The Way of the Rose* (Random House, 2019) pp. 110–111.

11. Morton M. Hunt, *The Natural History of Love* (Knopf, 1959) p. 24.

12. "Aphrodite," *Wikipedia*, https://en.wikipedia.org/wiki/Aphrodite.

13. Hunt, *The Natural History of Love*, p. 25.

14. Mark Cartwright, "Women in Ancient Greece," *World History Encyclopedia*, July 27, 2016, https://www.worldhistory.org/ article/927/women-in-ancient-greece.

15. Karen Armstrong, *A Short History of Myth* (Canongate, 2005).

16. Jalaja Bonheim, *Aphrodite's Daughters* (Fireside, 1997).

17. Nancy Qualls-Corbett, *The Sacred Prostitute* (Inner City, 1988).

18. Qualls-Corbett, *The Sacred Prostitute*, p. 39.

19. Stephanie Lynn Budin, *The Myth of Sacred Prostitution in Antiquity* (Cambridge University, 2008).

20. Mike Greenberg, "How to Pray to Aphrodite," Mythology Source, October 5, 2020, https://mythologysource.com/how-to-pray-to-aphrodite/.

Chapter 3

1. Nancy Qualls-Corbett, *The Sacred Prostitute* (Inner City, 1988).

2. Arianna Huffington, "The Gods of Greece," *Atlantic Monthly*, 1993, p. 60.

3. Huffington, "The God of Greece," pp. 64–66.

4. Jamake Highwater, *Myth & Sexuality* (New American Library, 1990) p. 86.

5. Julie Baumgold, "Fatale Attractions," *Vogue*, March 1998, p. 482, https://archive.vogue.com/article/1998/03/01/fatale-attractions.

6. Laura Kelly, "Character Archetypes: The Femme Fatale," ApolloPad, October 23, 2019, https://apollopad.com/blog/femme-fatale-archetype/.

7. Scott W. Stern, *The Trials of Nina McCall: Sex, Surveillance, and the Decades-Long Government Plan to Imprison "Promiscuous" Women* (Beacon, 2018).

8. Shere Hite, *The Hite Report* (Dell, 1976).

9. Monica Castillo, "The Disappearance of Shere Hite," RogerEbert.com, November 17, 2023, https://www.rogerebert.com/reviews/the-disappearance-of-shere-hite-movie-review-2023/.

10. Jean Shinoda Bolen, *Goddesses in Everywoman* (Harper, 2014); Jean Shinoda Bolen, *Gods in Everyman* (Harper, 2014); Agapi Stassinopoulous, *Gods and Goddesses in Love* (Paraview, 2004) p. 30; Jennifer Barker Woolger and Roger Woolger, *The Goddess Within* (Fawcett Columbine, 1989).

11. Arlene Diane Landau, *Tragic Beauty* (Chiron Publications, 2019).

Chapter 4

1. David R. Hawkins, *Power vs. Force: The Hidden Determinants of Human Behavior* (Hay House, 2002).

2. Viktor E. Frankl, *Man's Search for Meaning* (Washington Square Press, 1984) p. 86.

3. Frankl, *Man's Search for Meaning*, p. 86.

Chapter 5

1. Denis de Rougemont, *Love in the Western World*, trans. Montgomery Belgion (Pantheon, 1956) p. 64.

2. James Hillman, *Loose Ends* (Spring, 1994) p. 54.

3. Teresa of Avila, *Life of the Mother Teresa of Jesus* (1611) chapter XXIX, part 17.

4. C. S. Lewis, *The Four Loves* (Collins, 1960) pp. 87–89.

5. Caroline Knapp, *Appetites: Why Women Want* (Counterpoint, 2003) p. 89.

6. Arianna Huffington, "The Gods of Greece," *Atlantic Monthly*, 1993, p. 63.

7. Nancy Qualls-Corbett, *The Sacred Prostitute* (Inner City, 1988) p. 79.

8. Ginette Paris, *Pagan Meditations* (Spring, 1986) pp. 11–12.

9. Linda Kay Klein, "What Is Purity Culture?" https://lindakayklein. com/what-is-purity-culture/.

10. Susan Griffin, *The Book of the Courtesans* (Broadway, 2001) pp. 96–97.

11. Veronica Monet, *Sex Secrets of Escorts* (Alpha, 2005) p. 45.

12. Monet, *Sex Secrets of Escorts*, p. 261.

13. Eleanor Bertine, John Welwood ed., "The Alchemy of Man and Woman" in *Challenge of the Heart* (Shambala, 1985) pp. 140–141.

14. "Margot Anand," https://margotanand.com/.

15. M. Esther Harding, *The Way of All Women* (Harper Colophon, 1970) p. 300.

16. Lewis, *The Four Loves*, pp. 91–92.

17. Diane Ackerman, *A Natural History of the Senses* (Vintage, 1990) p. 59.

Chapter 6

1. Raymond Carver, *What We Talk About When We Talk About Love* (Vintage, 1989).

2. "Beauty," *Merriam-Webster*, https://www.merriam-webster.com/dictionary/beauty/.

3. John Keats, "Ode on a Grecian Urn," *Lamia, Isabella, The Eve of St. Agnes, and Other Poems*, https://www.poetryfoundation.org/poems/44477/ode-on-a-grecian-urn.

4. Roger Scruton, *Beauty* (Oxford University, 2011) p. 108.

5. Crispin Sartwell, "Beauty," *Stanford Encyclopedia of Philosophy*, March 22, 2022, https://plato.stanford.edu/entries/beauty/.

6. Denis Dutton, "A Darwinian Theory of Beauty," *TED*, February 2010, https://www.ted.com/talks/denis_dutton_a_darwinian_theory_of_beauty/.

7. Richard Seymour, "How Beauty Feels," *TED*, May 2011, https://www.ted.com/talks/richard_seymour_how_beauty_feels/.

8. Crispin Sartwell, *Six Names of Beauty* (Routledge, 2004) p. 57.

9. John-Mark L. Miravalle, *Beauty* (Sophia Institute, 2019) p. 4.

10. Gary Witherspoon, *Language and Art in the Navajo Universe* (University of Michigan, 1977) pp. 23–24.

11. Susan Magsamen, "Your Brain on Art: The Case for Neuroaesthetics," Cerebrum, July–August 2019, https://www.ncbi.nlm.nih.gov/pmc/articles/PMC7075503/.

12. "Neuroaesthetics," *Wikipedia*, February 27, 2024, https://en.wikipedia.org/wiki/Neuroesthetics#The_aesthetic_triad/.

13. David Konstan, *Beauty* (Oxford University, 2014).

14. "The Judgment of Paris in Greek Mythology," Greek Legends and Myths, https://www.greeklegendsandmyths.com/judgement-of-paris.html/.

15. Gary B. Meisner, *The Golden Ratio: The Divine Beauty of Mathematics* (RacePoint, 2018) pp. 76–77.

16. Sartwell, *Six Names of Beauty*, p. 114.

17. Alfred Tennyson, "Locksley Hall," *Poems* (1842).

18. John O'Donohue, *Beauty* (Harper Collins, 2004) p. 2.

Chapter 7

1. James Hillman, "The Practice of Beauty," *Uncontrollable Beauty*, eds. Bill Beckley and David Shapiro (Allworth, 1998) pp. 261–274.

2. Umberto Eco, "Umberto Eco on the Elusive Concept of Ugliness," *Literary Hub*, December 9, 2019, https://lithub.com/umberto-eco-on-the-elusive-concept-of-ugliness/.

3. Ann Sussman and Katie Chen, "The Mental Disorders that Gave Us Modern Architecture," *Common Edge*, August 22, 2017, https://commonedge.org/the-mental-disorders-that-gave-us-modern-architecture/.

4. Jennifer Gersten, "A Nordic Revolt Against 'Ugly' Modern Architecture," Bloomberg, August 1, 2023, https://www.bloomberg.com/news/features/2023-08-01/a-scandinavian-uprising-against-modern-architecture/.

5. Jane Evershed and Sacha Stone, "Modern Art: Conquest by Culture," *The Lazarus Initiative XXVI*, August 2023, https://lazarusinitiative.com/.

6. Evershed and Stone, "Modern Art."

7. Mark Devlin, *Musical Truth, Vol. 2*, (Asys, 2018) p. 187.

8. Simone Vitale, "423 Hz, A New Standard Pitch?" July 2016, https://soundofgoldenlight.com/432-hz/.

9. Devlin, *Musical Truth*.

10. "Vanity," *Merriam-Webster*, https://www.merriam-webster.com/dictionary/vanity/.

11. Andrew Smith, "The Venus Diary on the 12th of December," December 12, 2023, telegram.org/.

12. Henry David Thoreau, *Walden* (1854).

13. Hillman, "The Practice of Beauty," p. 263.

Chapter 8

1. Rachel Herz, *The Scent of Desire* (Harper Collins, 2007) p. 39.

2. Herz, *The Scent of Desire*, p. xv.

3. Marcel Proust, *In Search of Lost Time, Vol. 1: Swann's Way*, trans. C. K. Scott (Modern Library, 2003) p. 60.

4. Rudyard Kipling, "Lichtenberg," 1901, https://allpoetry.com/Lichtenberg/.

5. Diane Ackerman, *A Natural History of the Senses* (Vintage, 1990) p. 13.

6. Crispin Sartwell, *Six Names of Beauty* (Routledge, 2004) pp. 37–39.

7. "Song of Solomon 4": 9–15, https://biblehub.com/songs/.

8. Proust, *In Search of Lost Time*, pp. 63–64.

9. Epicurus, George K. Strondach trans., *The Art of Happiness* (Penguin Classics, 2012).

10. Masaru Emoto, *The Hidden Messages in Water* (Beyond Words, 2004).

11. Eric W. Dolan, "Listening to the Music You Love Will Make Your Brain Release More Dopamine, Study Finds," *PsyPost*, February 2, 2019, https://www.psypost.org/2019/02/listening-to-the-music-you-love-will-make-your-brain-release-more-dopamine-study-finds-53059/.

12. John Stuart Reid, "Sound Therapy: Medicine of the Future," Interview by Alec Sims, *The Shift Network*, https://theshiftnetwork.com/pak/47657/44106/.

13. "GNM Music (Mein Studentenmaedchen)," *New Medicine Online*, https://www.newmedicineonline.com/gnm-music/.

14. Anastasia Tsioulcas, "Struck with Memory Loss, A Dancer Remembers 'Swan Lake.' But Who Is She?" *NPR*, November 10, 2020, https://www.npr.org/2020/11/10/933387878/struck-with-memory-loss-a-dancer-remembers-swan-lake-but-who-is-she/.

15. Ackerman, *A Natural History of the Senses*, 191.

16. Kora Sevier, email to the author, August 9, 2023.

17. Dacher Kelter, "Hands on Research: The Science of Touch," *Greater Good Magazine*, September 29, 2010, https://greatergood.berkeley.edu/article/item/hands_on_research/.

18. Jonathan Jones, "Why Physical Touch Matters for Your Well-Being," *Greater Good Magazine*, November 16, 2018, https://greatergood.berkeley.edu/article/item/why_physical_touch_matters_for_your_well_being/.

19. Gabrielle Roth as interviewed by Cathleen Rountree, "Gabrielle Roth," *Coming into Our Fullness* (Crossing Press, 1991) p. 95.

Chapter 9

1. John Keats, "Eve of Saint Agnes," *Lamia, Isabella, the Eve of St. Agnes, and Other Poems* (1820) https://www.poetryfoundation.org/poems/44470/the-eve-of-st-agnes/.

2. Kumaradadatta, "Srngarakarika," https://www.exaltedmysticunion.com/mystical-verses.html.

3. Tony Richardson dir., *Tom Jones*, 1963, United Artists, 129 minutes.

4. William Shakespeare, *Macbeth*, Act 2, Scene 3, 1623.

5. Robert Fried and Lynn Edlen-Nezin, *Great Food, Great Sex* (Random House, 2006) p. 44.

6. D. H. Lawrence, "Figs," *Complete Poems* (Penguin, 1994), pp. 282–283.

Chapter 10

1. Laurelei Black, *Cult of Aphrodite* (Asteria, 2010).

2. Jalaja Bonheim, *Aphrodite's Daughters* (Fireside, 1997) p. 28.

3. Gary Witherspoon, *Language and Art in the Navajo Universe* (University of Michigan, 1977) p. 23.

4. Crispin Sartwell, *Six Names of Beauty* (Routledge, 2004) p. 135.

5. Mary Barnard trans., *Sappho* (University of California, 2019) p. 37.

Index

A

The Abuse of Beauty (Danto), 136
Ackermann, Diane (writer), 98, 146, 155
active ugliness, 123. *See also* ugliness
adlubescence, 133
Adonia festival, 41
Adonis, 39–41, 64
Adonis gardens, 41
Aeneas, 38
Aeschylus, 30, 86
aesthetics, 155
agape, 80
Age of Aquarius, 179–180
Agnes (author's mother)
    as Aphrodite's emissary on earth, 2
    comparing life with, 7
    gift of gardening, 5
    learning about love and beauty from, 7
    marriage, 6
    recollections of, 5–6
Alchemical Goddess, 69–70
alchemy, 54, 69
"The American Plan," 59
Anand, Margot (author), 93
Anathem (Stephenson), 121
Anchises, 38–39
anima, 57, 62
anima woman, 62
animus, 57
anise seeds, 171
anti-noise initiatives, 131

anxiety, 16
aphrodisiacs, 167–177
    alcohol, 173
    brief history of, 168–170
    chocolate, 174
    described, 167–168
    effectiveness of, 175–176
    foods that arouse the erotic imagina-
        tion as, 171
    fruits, 171
    herbs, 171
    non-food, 168
    nuts, 171
    seafood, 170–174
    spices, 171
    uses of, 168–169
    vegetable, 171
Aphrodisia festival, 46–47, 51
Aphrodite, 17–23
    Adonis, relationship with, 39–41, 64
    Anchises, relationship with, 38–39
    Ares, relationship with, 37, 42, 64
    author's affinity with, 2
    birth of, 33–34, 52
    declaration by, 30
    description of, 1–2
    evolution from ancient goddesses, 28
    goddesses beyond the power of, 64
    Great Awakening and, 17–23
    and the Judgement of Paris, 111

less flattering titles of, 54
myths of, 20–21, 31–45
as the Olympian Goddess of Love
    and Beauty, 25
overidentification with, 61–65
relationships with mortals, 38–41
relationships with Olympian deities,
    36–38
representation in other cultures, 26–27
sacred sexuality of, 85–90
symbols of, 35–36
titles of, 30–31
transformative powers of, 69–77
vengeful acts of, 54–56, 65
as a Virgin Goddess, 43
worship of, 45–52
Aphrodite-consciousness, 182–183, 184
Aphrodite of Knidos (sculpture), 45
Aphrodite Pandemos, 30–31
Aphrodite Urania, 30–31
Aphrodite-Venus, 2, 27, 28, 97, 113
apocalypse, 21
Apollo (God of the Sun), 26
ApolloPad (internet site), 59
Appetites: Why Women Want (Knapp), 83
apricity, 133
archetype of Aphrodite
    Great Awakening and, 184
    identifying with versus identifying
        as, 62
Architectural Uprising, 126–127
architecture, 124–127
The Architecture of Happiness (De Botton),
    110
Ares (God of War), 35, 36, 37, 40, 42, 64,
    93–95
Armstrong, Karen (comparative religion
    scholar), 19–20, 48
aroma, 149
aromatherapists, 147
art, ugliness in, 127–130
Artemis (Goddess of the Hunt), 26, 40,
    43, 64
ASD (autism spectrum disorder), 126

ASMR (Autonomous Sensory Meridian
    Response), 119
Asociación Música para Despertar
    (Music Association for
    Awakening), 154
Astarte, 28
Athena (Goddess of Wisdom and
    Crafts), 25, 43, 64, 111
Auden, W. H., 56
autism spectrum disorder (ASD), 126
Autonomous Sensory Meridian
    Response (ASMR), 119

B

Ballard, J. G., 11
Barnard, Maru, 188
"The Beautifier" (Sevier), 158
beauty, 101–120. *See also* ugliness
    in ancient Greece, 110–112
    of color, 156–159
    common associations with the word,
        102–103
    Darwinian theory of, 105
    definitions of, 102–106
    and exaltation of spirit, 106–109
    fashion and, 159–160
    golden ratio and, 112–115
    as guiding principle, 7
    listening to, 151–155
    longing for, 118–119
    objective view of, 103–104
    as one of Aphrodite's realms of influ-
        ence, 101–102
    power of, 6–7
    psychology of, 136–141
    reasons for not experiencing, 136–140
    scientific perspectives on, 108–109
    names for, 106
    skilled performance and perception of,
        105–106
    smell of, 144–148
    in sounds and music, 152–155

subjective view of, 104–105
taste of, 148–152
touch of, 160–162
ugliness as opposition to, 121–140
varied presence, 115–116
visual, 155–160
Beauty (goddess), 35
Beauty Diary, 76–77
beauty path, 75
Bergstresser, Ralph, 69
Bernini, Gian Lorenzo (sculptor), 81
Bertine, Eleanor, 91–92
bird symbols of Aphrodite, 36
The Birth of Venus (Botticelli), 113–114
Black, Laurelei (author), 181
body awareness, 164–166
Bolen, Jean Shinoda, 67, 70
Bonheim, Jalaja (author), 49, 181–182
Book of Revelation, 21
books, 162
Botticelli, Sandro, 113–114
Brooks, Geraldine, 9

C

Campbell, Joseph (mythologist), 28, 30
Carotenuto, Aldo, 51
Carson, Rachel, 115
Carver, Raymond (writer), 101
Castillo, Monica (film critic), 61
Catherine, Saint, 74
Chaos, 33
Chen, Katie, 126
chocolate, 174
"choosing one's own way," 73
Christian love, 80
chronic deprivation, 151
Cinyras, King of Cyprus, 39
Cleopatra (Queen of Egypt), 98–99
colors, 156–159
consultation process for, 158
cool, 157
emotion and physical effects of, 157
symbols of Aphrodite, 36

warm, 157
concert tuning, 131
conscious/ecstatic dance, 165
contemporary art, 128
Conti, Giovanna (music professor), 154
cool colors, 157. *See also* colors
Corinth, 46, 49
Cosmic Mother, 28
Cronus (Ruler of Time), 33, 52
cult centers, 46
Cult of Aphrodite (Black), 181
Cupid, 80
Cyprus, 33–34, 46, 52
Cythera, 46

D

damsel in distress, 59
The Danaides (Aeschylus), 32, 86
dance, 165
Danto, Arthur C., 136
Dark One, 54
"A Darwinian Theory of Beauty"
     (Dutton), 105
day symbol of Aphrodite, 36
De Botton, Alain (author), 110
Deceptive One, 54
De Divina Proportione (Pacioli), 114
Deimos (God of Terror), 37
deities, 25–26
Delilah, 58
Demeter (Goddess of the Harvest), 26,
     85–86
Demosthenes (statesman), 48
depression, 16
De Rougemont, Denis, 80
desires, 183–184
devadasis (servants of the Divine/Light),
     49
The Development of Personality (Jung), 57
Devlin, Mark (music historian), 131
Digby, Joan (author), 176
Digby, John (author), 176
dimpsy, 133

Dione, 32
Dionysus (God of Wine and Ecstasy), 37, 93–95
The Disappearance of Shere Hite (movie), 61
Divine Feminine, 2, 14–17, 86
    control of women's sexuality and, 88
    disconnection from, 14
    Divine Masculine and, 16–17
    energy, 9, 14–15, 33
    experiences of, 8
    Great Awakening and, 180
    secularization of sex and, 88
Divine Humans, 17
Divine Masculine energy, 15, 17, 86
Divine Mother, 28
The Double Flmae: Love and Eroticism (Paz), 93
Duchamp, Marcel, 128
Dutton, Denis, 105, 125

E

Earth, 33
earthing, 162
Earth-Mother, 86
éclats (rosy bursts of light), 90
Eco, Umberto (writer), 122
Emerson, Ralph Waldo, 187
Emoto, Masaru (author), 151
"Endymion" (Keats), 101
energy, 14
Epicurus, 150
equal temperament, 131
Erichthonius (son of Hephaestus and Gaia), 43
Eris (Goddess of Discord), 111
Eros (God of Love), 37, 39, 44, 55, 93
    origin of, 79
    role of, 79–80
eroticism, 93, 141–142
Euripides (playwright), 53, 57
Eve, 58
Evening Star, 27, 36

"Eve of Saint Agnes" (Keats), 169–170
Evershed, Jane (art historian), 127–128

F

fairy tales, 8
fashion, 159–160
fatal attraction, 58–61
femme fatale, 58–61
festivals, 41, 46–47
Fibonacci sequence, 114–115
Ficino, Marcello, 56
"Figs" (Lawrence), 176–177
Finn, Perdita, 43
Fisher, M. F. K., 167
5Rhythms movement, 165
Flowering (goddess), 35
flower symbols of Aphrodite, 36
foam-born, 34
Fomenko, Anatoly (mathematician), 22
food
    aphrodisiacs, 167–177
    aroma, 149
    chronic deprivation, 151
    expression of love with, 150
    taste of, 148–152
food deprivation, 151
Food for Thought (Digby), 176
forest bathing, 163–164
Fountain (Duchamp), 128
Frankl, Victor, 73
Franklin, Benjamin, 104
frequencies, 108
Freud, Sigmund, 80
Freya, 27
fruits, aphrodisiac, 171
fruit symbols of Aphrodite, 36

G

Gaia (Goddess of the Earth), 32–33
garlic, 171
The Gastronomical Me (Fisher), 167
German News Medicine (GNM), 154

girdle, 35
GNM (German News Medicine), 154
goddesses, 25–26. *See also* specific
    goddesses
  connection to the Great Goddess, 30
  overidentification with, 61–65
  role in love and seduction, 93–95
  virgin, 43
*Goddesses in Everywoman: A New
    Psychology of Women* (Bolen), 67, 70
Goddesses Never Age (Northrup), 183
Goddess of Destruction, 54
*The Goddess Within: A Guide to the Eternal
    Myths that Shape Women's Lives*
    (Woolger/Woolger), 67
gods, 26
  role in love and seduction, 93–95
*Gods and Goddesses in Love: Making
    the Myth a Reality for You*
    (Stassinopoulos), 67
*Gods in Everyman: A New Psychology of
    Men's Lives and Loves* (Bolen), 67
Golden Age, 180
Golden Apple, 111–112
golden girdle, 35
Golden Goddess. *See* Aphrodite
Golden One, 53–54, 66
golden ratio (golden proportion),
    112–115
*The Golden Ratio: The Divine Beauty of
    Mathematics* (Meisner), 113
Gonzales, Martina, 154
Gordon, J. E. (author), 123
Graces (goddesses), 34–35
Great Awakening, 179–189
  about, 12–14
  Age of Aquarius and, 179–180
  Aphrodite and, 17–23
  Aphrodite-consciousness and, 182–
    183, 184
  desires and, 183–184
  dissolution of beliefs about reality
    in, 13
  Divine Feminine and, 9, 180

Navajo people and, 184–186
Greater Good Science Center, 161
Great Food, Great Sex, 175
Great Goddess, 28, 29, 41, 43
Great Mother Goddess, 28, 40, 43, 44,
    180
Greek mythology, origin of, 28
grounding, 162
Growth (goddess), 35

H

Harding, M. Esther, 96
Harmonia (Goddess of Harmony), 37
Harris, Joan (author), 174
Harrison, Jane Ellen (anthropologist), 29
Hathor, 27
Hawkins, David R., 71–72
healing, 13
health problems, 16
Hedone, 82
Helen of Troy, 111–112
Hellenic period, 29
Hephaestus (God of the Forge), 5–6, 35,
    41–42, 85
Hera (Goddess of Marriage)., 6, 26, 35,
    85, 111
herbs, aphrodisiac, 171
Hermaphroditos (bisexual son of
    Aphrodite), 37
Hermes (Messenger of the Gods), 26,
    36–37
Herophilos (daughter of Aphrodite), 37
hertz, 131
Herz, Rachel (author), 144
Hesiod (poet), 32, 33
Hestia (Goddess of the Hearth), 43, 64
hetaerae (courtesans), 47–48, 49
The Hidden Messages in Water (Emoto),
    151
hieros gamos (mystical marriage), 86
Hildegard, Saint, 14–15, 179
Hillman, James (psychologist), 18, 57,
    137–138, 163

Hippolytus (Euripides), 53, 57
Hippolytus (prince of Troizenus), 54, 57
history, 21–23
Hite, Shere, 60–61
The Hite Report: A National Study of Female Sexuality (Hite), 60
hochxq, 185
The Holy Virgin Mary (Ofili), 129
Homer, 25, 29, 38
"Homeric Hymn to Aphrodite" (Homer), 25, 38
honor culture, 88
Horowitz, Len (author/health advocate), 132
Housden, Roger, 141
"How Beauty Feels" (Seymour), 105
hozho, 106, 107–108, 184–186. *See also* beauty
Huffington, Arianna (author), 56
Hume, David, 104
Hungerford, Margaret, 104

I

Iliad (Homer), 29
Inanna, 28
individuation, 69–70
Ingrid (author's neighbor)
    affair with Jack, 4
    babysitting for, 4–5
    comparing life with, 7–8
    learning about the power of beauty from, 6–7
    recollections of, 3–4
international modernism, 125
International Organization for Standardization, 131
international style, 125
intuition, 142, 182
involuntary memory, 145
Ishtar, 28
Isis, 28
I Spy (game), 156
Itten, Johannes, 158

J

Joy (goddess), 35
The Joy of Painting (television show), 119
"The Judgment of Paris," 110–111
Jung, Carl, 8, 57, 70, 84–85, 86
just intonation, 131

K

kallos, 110–111
kalon, 106. *See also* beauty
Kant, Immanuel, 103–104
Keats, John (poet), 58, 101, 103, 169
Keller, Helen, 155
Kelter, Dacher, 161
Kidman, Nicole (actress), 61
Killer of Men, 54
Kipling, Rudyard, 145
Klein, Linda Kay, 88
Kluckhohn, Clyde, 107–108
Knapp, Caroline, 83–84
Knidos (ancient Greek city), 45
Konstan, David, 110
Kumaradadatta, 170
Kunst der Farbe (Itten), 158
Kythira, 46

L

"La Belle Dame sans Merci" (Keats), 58
lady of Kypros. *See* Aphrodite
"laicized sex" (secularized sex), 87
Landau, Arlene Diane (psychotherapist), 62, 67
language, ugliness in, 132–134
Language and Art in the Navajo Universe (Witherspoon), 185–186
Lawrence, D.H., 176–177
Le Corbusier (architect), 126
legends, 8
legumes, 171
Lesbos, 22

Les Demoiselles d'Avignon (Picasso), (painting), 128
Leto (Greek Goddess of Motherhood), 5
Lewis, C. S. (writer), 82, 96–97
Libra (astrological sign), 2
"Lichtenberg" (Kipling), 145
life energy, 80
life instinct, 80
logarithmic scale, 73
love, 62
    expressing, 74
    food and expression of, 150
    as guiding principle, 7
    between the same sex, 91–92
    and senses, 142–143
love frequency, 132
Love in the Western World (de Rougement), 80
lovers, compatibility of, 95

M

Macbeth (Shakespeare), 162
Magsamen, Susan (researcher), 109
mainstream media, 16
Man's Search for Meaning (Frankl), 73
Mark Anthony (Roman general), 98–99
marriage, in ancient Greece, 48
masculine energy, 15
Mata Hari, 58
Meisner, Gary B., 113–114
Menelaus (King of Sparta), 111–112
mental disorder, 125–126
mineral symbols of Aphrodite, 36
Miravalle, John-Mark (Christian scholar), 107
mirrors, as symbol of Aphrodite, 36
mistresses, 48
modern art, 127–128
modernism, 125
moicheia, 48
Molly Bawn (Hungeford), 105
Monet, Veronica, 90
Monroe, Marilyn (actress), 62

Mormons, 88
Morning Star, 27, 36, 135
Mother Earth, 14, 33
multisensory experience, 163–164
music *See also* sound
    beauty of, 152–155
    healing effects of, 154
Music Association for Awakening, 154
Muslims, 88
Myrrha, 39
mystical marriage, 86
myths, 8, 18–21

N

Nature and Other Writings (Emerson), 187
Navajo-Diné, 75
Navajo people, 107–108, 184–186
negative masculine energy, 15
Nerites (nymph and lover of Aphrodite), 54
neuroaesthetics, 109
New Chronology movement, 22
New Earth, 180
noise, 131
Northrup, Christiane, 183
nuts, aphrodisiac, 171

O

Object to Be Destroyed (Ray), 128
"Ode on a Grecian Urn" (Keats), 103
O'Donohue, John, 118
odor association, 143
Odyssey (Homer), 29
Ofili, Chris, 129
olfactory glands, 144
olives, 171
original sin, 16
overidentification with Aphrodite, 61–65
    anima woman and, 62–63
    effects of, 61–62

emotional powerless in love and,
63–64
identifying with versus identifying as
archetype, 62
principle of eros and, 63
oysters as aphrodisiac, 171–172

P

Pacioli, Luca, 114
Paphos, 34
Paris (Prince of Troy), 111–112
Paris, Ginette (social psychologist), 87,
89
Pausinias (writer), 51
Paz, Octavio, 93
Peitho (Goddess of Charming Speech
and Persuasion), 31, 37, 134
Peleus, 111
perfume, 147
Pericles (statesman), 47
Persephone (Goddess of the
Underworld), 39–40
petrichor, 133
Phaedra (stepmother of Hippolytus), 54
Phaedrus (Plato), 79
Phobos (God of Fear), 37
physical beauty, disruptive power of, 6–7
Picasso, Pablo, 128
Piccinini, Patricia (artist), 129
pitch, 131–132
Plato, 30, 79, 103
Pleasure, 82
Plotinus, 103, 121, 137–138
pomegranates, 171
pornai (profane or secular prostitutes), 50
pornography, 86–87
Poseidon (God of the Sea), 26, 37
post-traumatic stress disorder (PTSD),
126
pothos, 81
*Power vs. Force: The Hidden Determinants
of Human Behavior* (Hawkins), 71
The Practice of Beauty (Hillman), 18, 163

Praxiteles (sculptor), 45
Priapos, 37
priestesses, as sacred prostitutes, 49
proprioception, 142
prostitution, 47–48, 50
Proust, Marcel, 145, 149
Proust effect, 145
Psyche, 55, 82
Ptolemies, 98
PTSD (post-traumatic stress disorder),
126
purity movement, 88

Q

Qualls-Corbett, Nancy (author), 50
quinces, 171–172

R

Radiance (goddess), 35
Ray, Man, 128
Reichard, Gladys (anthropologist),
184–185
Reid, John Stuart (acoustics scientist),
154
Renaissance Period, 89
Renold, Maria (musician), 132
Revelation, 21
Rhodos (daughter of Aphrodite), 37
Rites and Myths of Seduction
(Carotenuto), 51
Rockefeller Foundation, 131
roses, as Aphrodite's signature flower, 5,
40, 146
Ross, Bob (painter), 119–120
Roth, Garbrielle (dancer), 165

S

Sacred Feminine energy, 14
sacred prostitutes, 48–50, 89
sacred sexuality, 85–90
Salome, 58

Sappho (poet), 22–23, 89, 188
Sartwell, Crispin, 106, 115–116, 146
Scivias (Saint Hildegard of Bingen),
    14–15, 179
Scruton, Roger, 103
seafood, aphrodisiac, 171
seashells, as symbol of Aphrodite, 36
secularized sex, 87–88
seduction, 92–93
The Sense of Wonder (Carson), 115
senses, 142–143
    body awareness, 164–166
    multisensory experience, 163–164
    odor association, 143
    proprioception, 142
    smells, 144–148
    taste, 148–152
    touch, 160–162
    vestibular, 142–143
sensory receptors, 161
servants of the Divine/Light, 49
Sevier, Kora (architectural color consul-
    tant), 158
sex
    Aphrodite and, 44
    secularization of, 87–88
Sex Secrets of Escorts: Tips from a Pro
    (Monet), 90
sexuality, 44
    purity movement and, 88
    religion and, 88
    sacred, 85–90
    "social hygiene" campaign and, 59–60
sexual priestesses, 48–50
sexual relationships
    appreciation of own body in, 97–98
    compatibility of lovers in, 95
    gods associated with, 93–95
Seymour, Richard, 105–107
Shakespeare, William, 104, 174
Shakti, 86
Shape magazine, 83
shinrin-yoku (forest bathing), 163–164
Shiva, 86

shrines, 30
sin, 16
Singstad, Kurt (architect), 127
Six Names for Beauty (Sartwell), 106
skin, 160–161
Sky-Father, 86
smells, 144–148. *See also* senses
Smith, Andrew (astrologer), 135
"social hygiene" campaign, 59–60
Song of Solomon, 147–148
Soul and Sensuality (Housden), 141
sound. *See also* music; senses
    absence of, 154–155
    beauty of, 152–155
    ugliness in, 130–132
Spetnak, Chalene (scholar), 34
spices, aphrodisiac, 171
Spillane, Mickey, 59
spirituality, development of, 8
spring, 36, 116–117
Sri Lakshmi, 27
"Srngarakarika," 170
Stassinopoulos, Agapi (author), 42, 67
Stephenson, Neal (author), 121
Strand, Clark, 43
*Structures: Or Why Things Don't Fall
    Down* (Gordon), 123
Summer Solstice, 46
sundara, 106. *See also* beauty
supraordinate third energy, 86
Sussman, Ann, 126
Swan Lake (Tchaikovsky), 154
Swann's Way (Proust), 145
symbols of Aphrodite, 35–36
Symbols of Transformation (Jung), 84–85
Symposium (Plato), 30

T

tai chi, 165
Tantra, 93
taste, 148–152. *See also* senses
Tchaikovsky, Pyotr Ilyich (composer),
    154

TED Talk, 105
television, 16
Temple of Aphrodite, 45
temples, 45, 48–51, 89
Tennyson, Alfred, 116
Teresa of Avila, 81–82
Tesla, Nikola, 69
thanatos (death instinct/drive), 80
Theias, King of Assyria, 39
Theseus (father of Hippolytus), 54
Thetis, 111
thiasos, 22, 89
Thomas Aquinas, Saint, 103
Thoreau, Henry David, 137
tirliry-pufkin, 133
Tom Jones (movie), 172
touch, 160–162. *See also* senses
Tragic Beauty (Landau), 62, 67
transformative process, 70–74
transport symbols of Aphrodite, 36
trauma, 125–126
Trojan War, 112
tuning pitch, 131–132

U

ugliness, 121–140. *See also* beauty
    active, 123
    as antithesis to beauty, 121
    in architecture, 124–127
    in art, 127–130
    in language, 132–134
    in sound, 130–132
    in vanity, 134–136
umami, 149
Underworld, 40
Unholy One, 54
Upperworld, 40
Uranus (God of the Sky or Heaven),
    32, 52

V

Valentine's Day, 168
vanity, 134–136
vegetable, aphrodisiac, 171
Venus, 1, 135
Venus (planet), 2, 27, 36
Venus (Roman Goddess of Love), 27
Venus-Aphrodite, 2, 27, 28, 97, 113
vestibular senses, 142–143
vibrational frequencies, 108
virgin, 43
Virgin Goddesses, 43

W

wabi-sabi, 106, 115–116, 157. *See also*
    beauty
warm colors, 157. *See also* colors
The Way of the Rose (Strand/Finn), 43
Weiwei, Ai (artist), 129
"What We Talk About When We Talk
    About Love" (Carver), 101
Witherspoon, Gary (author), 185–186
Woolger, Jennifer Baker, 67
Woolger, Roger, 67
worship of Aphrodite, 45–52
worthiness, 88

Y

yapha, 106, 146. *See also* beauty
yoga, 165
You Know The Place: Then (Sappho), 189

Z

Zeki, Semir (neurobiologist), 109
Zeus (God of the Sky and Thunder and
    Ruler of the Olympians), 26, 29,
    35, 38, 40, 85

About the Author

Geraldine S. Brooks is a writer, researcher, and psychologist.

As a writer and researcher, Geraldine focuses on the topics of personal and spiritual development, Divine Feminine consciousness, the transformative powers of love and beauty, and mind/body healing. As a psychologist, she takes an integrative approach informed by scientific advances in psychology, as well as the wisdom of many traditional Western and Eastern health disciplines.

She received her PhD from the University of British Columbia in Counseling Psychology and has also pursued advanced formal education in Jungian, Transpersonal, and Energy Psychologies, as well as informal studies in a variety of esoteric and holistic health-related subjects.

She currently lives and works in Vancouver, BC.

For updates on Geraldine's publications and events,
as well as more information about Aphrodite,
the Divine Feminine, love, and beauty, please visit
www.geraldinesbrooks.com

From joy springs all creation
By it is sustained,
Towards joy it proceeds
And to joy it returns.

—VEDIC TEXT, *MUNDAKA UPANISHAD*

www.ingramcontent.com/pod-product-compliance
Lightning Source LLC
Chambersburg PA
CBHW020447130626
46549CB00001B/333